A Discipled Nation Series

The MASTER'S PLAN for YOU

JIM DYET
JIM RUSSELL

A Discipled Nation Book ®

The Amy Foundation, P.O. Box 16091, Lansing, Michigan
48901.

Cover, text design, and typography: Ragont Design.

ISBN 1-931774-30-0

Printed in the United States of America

CONTENTS

PREFACE

When our house was under construction, my wife and I drove past the site at least once a week. From groundbreaking to walk through, we followed the progress and at times the regress. For example, the framing regressed. It failed inspection and had to be brought up to code. Later, my wife told me she was certain the builders had framed the dining room for a flat window instead of the bay window we had ordered and paid extra for. Sure enough, she was right. Back to the drawing board! The wiring regressed too. First, the wires to the dishwasher and the garbage disposal were crossed. Were we supposed to put our dishes in the garbage disposal and our food scraps in the dishwasher? A telephone jack was installed upside down and another was missing altogether. Also, a kitchen outlet kept tripping. I won't get into the plumbing situation. Suffice to say, mistakes were corrected. Now we live in a house properly framed, with a dining room bay window, functional dishwasher and garbage disposal, and water where it is supposed to be instead of where it isn't supposed to be.

If only the contractor and sub-contractors had followed the master plan! Everything would have gone faster and better, and everyone would have been happy.

In life, as in our experience with construction, failure to follow a plan leads inevitably to disappointment and loss. But whose plan is perfect? Certainly not yours or mine! Not even the best financial planner can control the variables that impact the economy. Nor can the most knowledgeable counselor provide flawless guidance. More than one multi-millionaire has seen his or her fortune implode and vanish into thin air. And many a soul marching energetically toward his life's goals, has encountered a roadblock or a detour leading to catastrophic illness or long-term unemployment. If one thing is certain about our self-laid plans, it is that nothing is certain about them.

Nevertheless, one plan exists that will not—cannot—fail. It is the Master's plan for you. Jesus, the Good Shepherd and our Master, promised that He walks ahead of His sheep, calls them by name, and leads them (John 10:3, 4). What better direction in life could anyone possibly take than the one charted by the all-knowing, all-loving Savior? He leads His followers along the path of blessing, where peace and joy flourish like rain-watered flowers. Along the way, He gives us the privilege of introducing others to Him so they can follow Him too. When the journey ends, we will step inside heaven, where eternal bliss, endless joy, and incomparable rewards await us.

To a great extent the Master's plan for you and me is precisely the one He followed when He visited Planet Earth two millennia ago. The plan was to make disciples and pour His life into theirs. So He often took them away from the crowds for close-up and personal training. He schooled them in God's ways. He demonstrated the life that pleases God. He showed them what selfless love and compassion are. He assured them that He possesses all authority in heaven and on earth, and He commanded them to go, supported by His authority, and make disciples.

It is my prayer and Jim Russell's prayer that this book will help you make disciples and enjoy the unparalleled blessings that accompany the Master's plan for you.

—JIM DYET

Chapter One

COMPLETE
FORGIVENESS
& FREEDOM

" . . .with liberty and justice for all." Sweet words, aren't they? But when we pledge allegiance to our flag and country, do we consider the price many have paid to protect and preserve our liberty and justice? Brave men and women have fought and even died to keep our nation free and just. Because of their sacrifices, we can choose our own political leaders; we can decide where we will live and work, where we will travel, and how we will spend our income.

It's hard to imagine life without freedom. Picture the two American young women held captive for weeks in Afghanistan. The Taliban had arrested Heather Mercer and Dayna Curry for sharing Bible stories about Jesus. Just before their rescue, the two were huddled in a cold steel container thinking it might be their last night alive.

Or picture the plight of a Colorado boy who lived from age 9 to 11 in a 12-by-12 concrete room in the family home. The room held only a chair, a small desk, and a sleeping bag. Plywood covered its only window and an alarm sounded whenever he tried to open the door. His parents punished him for misbehaving by confining him to "the hole," a 16-square-foot, dark concrete space under a flight of stairs that was also armed with an alarm. The cell had only a blanket and a bucket. He was released from confinement just one hour a day. Fortunately, Heather and Dayna were freed after the Taliban had fled the city in which they were incarcerated, and the cruelly treated boy was rescued from his unnatural existence. In each situation, the newfound freedom must have felt similar to how a deep breath of fresh air feels to a person rescued from drowning.

Only the freedom enjoyed by Jesus' followers exceeds the value of personal freedom. It reaches beyond human comprehension and extends through time and eternity. It includes forgiveness, peace with God, and the power to lead a righteous life. Jesus categorized all men and women as either slaves to sin or liberated from sin.

JESUS BRINGS FORGIVENESS AND FREEDOM

The eighth chapter of John's Gospel unfolds two stories that spotlight the liberating power of Jesus' forgiveness and teachings. The first features a woman enslaved by sin until Jesus set her free. The second features a group of religious people enslaved by their self-righteous attitude.

The woman in the first story ranked extremely low in society's eyes. She had been caught in the act of adultery and dragged by zealous religious leaders to the temple, where Jesus was teaching. Bent on ridding society of this immoral woman, the religious leaders prepared to stone her to death, and they pressured Jesus to weigh in on their decision. His response was unexpected. He stooped down and started writing on the ground—perhaps the chief sins of the woman's accusers. For a while, the religious leaders continued to question Jesus, "If any one of you is without sin," Jesus challenged, "let him be the first to throw a stone at her." Again, he stooped down and wrote on the ground. When he stood up, He found that one by one the accusers had slipped away. Only He and the guilty woman remained.

"Woman, where are they? Has no one condemned you?" He asked.

"No one, sir," she replied.

"Then neither do I condemn you," Jesus announced. "Go now and leave your life of sin."

Jesus' liberating forgiveness staggers the mind, doesn't it? He not only forgave a woman whom society disdained, but He also let her know He expected her to live differently—free to be the woman God wanted her to be. He had accepted her just as He found her, but He did not leave her as He had found her. He lifted her from a low life to a life of high potential. He elevated her from wretchedness to righteousness, from disaster to dignity, from shame to self-respect, from sin to significance, and from perversion to privilege.

We must not misjudge the liberty Jesus gives His followers. We must not mistake it as a license to do whatever we please. Rather, liberty enables us to do whatever pleases our Lord. We are free to choose to do right and empowered to resist the temptation to do what is wrong. Friedrich von Hayek wrote about civil liberty in "The Constitution of Liberty," 1960. He observed: "Liberty not only means that the individual has both the opportunity and the burden of choice; it also means that he must bear the consequences of his actions. Liberty and responsibility are inseparable." The same principle applies to spiritual liberty: Those whom Jesus sets free are responsible for their actions. Freedom of choice leads to consequences. If we choose to live righteously, we will enjoy the rewards of a righteous life; if we choose to sin willfully, we will experience shame, regret, and unrest.

Many passages of Scripture emphasize the need to assume a high view of divine grace, but two are especially significant. Romans 6:1 underscores the shame of viewing God's grace as cheap and a license to sin. Titus 2:11-14 points out the importance of being motivated by His grace to live for His honor.

Romans 6:1: "What shall we say, then? Shall we go on sinning so that grace may increase? By no means! We died to sin; how can we live in it any longer?"

Titus 2:11-14: "For the grace of God that brings salvation has appeared to all men. It teaches us to say "No" to ungodliness and worldly passions, and to live self-controlled, upright and godly lives in this present age, while we wait for the blessed hope—the glorious appearing of our great

God and Savior, Jesus Christ, who gave himself for us to redeem us from all wickedness and to purify for himself a people that are his very own, eager to do what is right."

Many of Jesus' 21st-century followers can identify with the adulterous woman whom Jesus set free from sin. Previously enslaved to sexual immorality or drugs or a violent temper or lying or a life of crime or some other form of wickedness, they experienced Jesus' compassion, forgiveness and liberating power. Now they serve and obey Him. Righteousness, love, mercy, and kindness characterize their lives, and praise and thanksgiving ascend from their hearts and lips to their new Master. They understand what prompted a songwriter to write

> "Saved by His power divine,
> Saved to new life sublime.
> Life now is sweet, and my joy is complete
> For I'm saved, saved, saved."

The second story in John, chapter 8, reports a conversation between Jesus and a number of self-righteous Jews, who claimed to accept Jesus' teachings but had no intention of following Him. Jesus explained that His true disciples obey His teachings, which He characterized as the truth. If the Jews would hold to His teachings, they would know the truth and it would set them free, He promised (verse 32). But the Jews responded by denying that they needed to be set free. They boasted that they had a religious pedigree that stretched all the way back to Abraham, the founding father of Israel. They assumed they were acceptable to God because they had been members of Abraham's family since birth. However, as Jesus explained, a big difference exists between being born into a certain family or religion and being born into God's family. As He had pointed out to Nicodemus, a ruler of the Jews, membership in God's family requires a spiritual birth (see John 3:3-8).

Jesus' words leave no doubt that forgiveness and freedom to be what God wants us to be and to do what He wants us to do are not products of religious affiliation or religious fervor. We do not become God's children by

- being born in the United States;
- residing in a Christian nation;
- being baptized;
- joining a church;
- having Christian parents;
- being related to a minister;
- giving to charity;
- attending church regularly;
- taking communion;
- leading a respectable life.

Although we may value the items in the preceding list, we must understand in light of Jesus' teaching that none of them can gain God's forgiveness and free us from our sin. Jesus earned our forgiveness and freedom by dying on the cross for us, and He grants both to whoever believes on Him and becomes His follower.

FORGIVENESS IS MEANT TO BE SHARED

As Jesus taught and ministered to the human condition during the three and a half years that intervened between His baptism and crucifixion, He forgave many men and women and set them free to be what God wanted them to be. But He also taught the forgiven to be forgiving. Addressing His disciples, Jesus said, "If your brother sins, rebuke him, and if he repents, forgive him. If he sins against you seven times in a day, and seven times comes back to you and says, 'I repent,' forgive him" (Luke 17:3). Tall order, but the same grace Jesus extends in forgiving us works in us effectively to help us forgive others.

A mother who became a follower of Jesus learned firsthand how difficult, but important, it can be to forgive an offender. She came face to face with the man who had raped and murdered her 20-year-old daughter. The meeting was not by accident. The mother had arranged to visit the murderer in prison. But as she sat in a visitation cell and looked across a plain wooden table and into the face of the man who had robbed her of the special joy that accompanies a mother-daughter relationship, she choked for a moment or two. How could she say, "I forgive you"? This was the man who had snuffed out the life of her daughter. Then she remembered that Jesus had forgiven all her sins. Struggling to mouth the words, but keeping a steady voice, she told her daughter's murderer, "I could have written a letter and mailed it to you, but I wanted to come here today and tell you in person that I forgive you."

Granted, it may be extremely difficult to forgive those who have hurt us, but it may hurt us more not to forgive. Bitterness toward our offenders can eat at us while our hatred boils, our irritability builds, our joy vanishes, and our relationships sour. Exercising forgiveness empowers us to release bitterness as we might release a helium-filled balloon into a blue sky. Having forgiven our offenders, we can get on with the business of living. We can recapture joy, grip God's peace, and build satisfying relationships.

Jack was the kind of employee others liked to work with. He had a smile for everyone, shouldered his responsibility, was a team player, and sported a good disposition. No one was surprised to see Jack promoted through the ranks and become the CEO's right-hand man. But Jack soon found himself in the unenviable role of hatchet man when the company faced economic challenges. Although he knew the cash flow was still healthy but not as healthy as it had been, Jack carried out the boss's orders to cut salaries and lay off long-time employees. He was also ordered to call the employees together and tell them the cash flow had dried up and the company was operating in the red. At the same time he saw the CEO's salary increase dramatically, with an increasing number of perks and bonuses.

Jack's disposition changed. He became moody, irritable, and ill. Going to work was no longer something to anticipate; it had become a nightmare. Bitterness toward the CEO welled up in Jack's soul. He felt used and betrayed. How could the CEO cast him into such a miserable role?

One day, after lunch, Jack told the CEO how he felt. He submitted his resignation, walked out of the building, and never returned.

For months Jack stewed over the hurt he believed the CEO had inflicted on him. He became so depressed that he could not even apply for a new job. He stopped attending church because he felt God had let him down. He moped around the house and grew distant from his wife and children.

Then, one day, a Christian friend advised Jack that harboring resentment was hurting him and his loved ones, not the CEO. "God wants you to repent of bitterness, forgive, and start fresh in your relationships—with Him and others," the friend said straight out. "When you forgive, you will feel that a ton of bricks has been lifted from your soul."

Jack took the advice, repented, forgave the CEO, and experienced the liberating power of Jesus. Free from bitterness, irritability, depression, and sulking, Jack regained his pleasant disposition, experienced joy and peace, renewed a close relationship with his family, and got a new job. Today, Jack is happily retired; prosperous, and quick to tell others that forgiveness is a big part of the Lord's prescription for a happy life.

The Perfect Model for Forgiving Others

The greatest demonstration of forgiveness occurred on Mount Calvary, outside Jerusalem, when Jesus was dying on the cross. Although wicked minds had plotted His death, wicked hands had nailed Him to the cross, and wicked insults were hurled at Him, Jesus prayed, "Father, forgive them, for they do not know what they are doing" (Luke 23:34). Such forgiveness sets a high but attainable standard for all who claim to follow Jesus. The standard is high because it is divine. It is attainable because Jesus rose from the dead and enables His followers to obey His commands.

The apostle Paul caught the essence of the forgiveness Jesus extended to His murderers, and he encouraged believers to adopt it as the model for forgiving others. He wrote in Colossians 3:13: "Bear with each other, and forgive whatever grievances you may have against one another, Forgive as the Lord forgave you."

Here are a few suggested helps for forgiving others:

- Recall that you did not deserve the Lord's forgiveness.

- Reflect upon the unconditional love the Lord showered upon you by dying for your sins and forgiving you.

- Be aware that your forgiving others is an act of loving obedience to the Lord.

- Realize that forgiving those who have hurt you as an opportunity to share the Lord's love with them.

- Understand that unwillingness to forgive hurts you more than the offenders.

- Seize the opportunity to forgive others as one in which you strengthen your relationship with the Lord and heal broken human relationships.

A grudge is the heaviest load anyone can carry through life. The Lord has made it possible for us to cast the load aside and walk unencumbered in the path of righteousness. Forgiven followers of Jesus who forgive others know the truth and live free!

Interactive Discipleship

ANSWER THE FOLLOWING QUESTIONS:

1. What do you think following Jesus involves?

2. Do you consider yourself a follower of Jesus?

3. If you are His follower, how can you show you are grateful He has forgiven you?

4. If you are not Jesus' follower, will you believe on Him now and become His follower?

5. How can a person know that his or her sins have been forgiven?

6. Why is it possible to be religious but also a slave to sin?

7. Do you agree or disagree that someone may have sinned too grievously to be forgiven? Why or why not?

8. Suggest four adjectives that characterize the truth Jesus taught.

9. How might freedom from sin's power change someone's life for the good?

10. How will you share the message of Jesus' forgiveness and liberating power with someone this week?

READ WHAT THE FOLLOWING PASSAGES SAY ABOUT FORGIVENESS AND FREEDOM:

Genesis 50:15-21; Psalms 32; 103; Micah 7:18, 19; Matthew 18:21-35; Acts 13:32-39; Ephesians 2:1-10; I John 1:1-10; Revelation 1:1-5

MAKE DISCIPLES.

- Share this chapter with a friend.
- Tell a friend how you received forgiveness.
- Discuss what it means to be truly free.
- Help your friend decide to follow Jesus.
- Encourage your friend to confront bitterness and seek the Lord's assistance in forgiving others.
- Select one of the Scripture passages cited above, and suggest to your friend that you read it together.
- Pray that you and your friend will be able to forgive others and live free from sin's power.

MULL IT OVER.

How complete is divine forgiveness? According to Psalm 103:12, when the Lord forgives us, He casts our sins as far from us as the east is from the west. North meets south at the South Pole, and south meets north at the North Pole; but east and west never meet. Just as we will never find either an East Pole or a West Pole, so we will never find the sins the Lord has removed from us. They are gone forever. Now, that's complete forgiveness!

LOVE TO
ENJOY
AND SHARE

Psychologist Abraham Maslow included the need
to be loved in his hierarchy of basic human needs.
Who would disagree? From infancy to old age, human beings need to feel loved. Unloved, we hurt.
Our self-esteem tumbles, our sense of security
crumbles, and our ability to relate to others stum-
bles. Whenever we hear that a newborn has been
abandoned, we cringe. We ask, "How could anyone cast aside a helpless little baby?" When a parent abuses a child, we wonder what kind of
monster could do that. When we learn that a
spouse has abused his or her partner, we remon-
strate. We wonder what destroyed the love that was
pledged at the marriage altar. How did the relationship turn so ugly? Our minds reel whenever we
hear about a terrorist attack at home or abroad. It
is almost inconceivable that so much hate plagues

our times. What might it take for love to displace hate?

No Substitute for Real Love

Before we understand what real love is, we must identify counterfeit love. Otherwise, we may settle for far less than the love God demands. He commanded: "Love the LORD your God with all your heart and with all your soul and with all your strength" and "love your neighbor as yourself" (Deuteronomy 6:5; Leviticus 19:18). This love involves our whole being, so anything less is hypocritical. We do not truly love God if we pay Him only lip service on Sunday morning. Nor do we truly love our neighbor if we merely say "Hi" but close our eyes to his needs. The love God demands is pure, so anything less than pure is counterfeit. We do not truly love God if we esteem material goods or another person more highly than God. Even love of self fails the test of true love unless it ranks under love for God and others. Love of self must reflect an appreciation of God's love for us and carry the conviction that our every personal asset is a gift of His grace.

Erotic love is not true love. Nor is mere physical attraction true love. Movies may define love in these ways, but the Bible defines love as a self-sacrificing, all-consuming emotion that puts the interests of God and others ahead of our own interests. Love that depends upon physical attraction usually slips away when wrinkles appear or hair turns gray. It can't comprehend the sentiment expressed in the words of an old song: "When your hair has turned to silver, I will love you just the same." Mere physical love often goes stale before the wedding cake does. A marriage built only on physical attraction has no hope of celebrating a 50th Anniversary. Fifty days. Yes. Fifty months. Perhaps. But 50 years. No way!

Nor is just liking someone real love. We may like someone because he or she is easy to like but dislike another person because he or she tries our patience and frays our nerves. Jesus commanded, "Love your enemies. Do good to those who hate you, bless those who curse you, pray for those who mistreat you" (Luke 6:27, 28).

Tony and Brad are best friends. They work as salesmen for the same car dealership and have common interests: fishing, golf, football, and restoring antique automobiles. They like each other mainly because they both like the same things. But Tom and Brad are anything but fond of Cory, who is also a salesman at the dealership. Cory comes across as aggressive, rude, and boisterous. He pounces on potential customers before they walk into the showroom. He grabs them before they have a chance to meet any of the other sales people. He even steals customers who ask specifically for Tony or Brad. He badmouths competitors and lies about delivery dates, anticipated gas mileage, and warranty coverage. To make matters worse, he mocks Tony and Brad's enjoyment of "chasing a little white ball around a golf course," "drowning worms," and watching "Monday Night Foolsball."

Whenever possible Tony and Brad avoid Cory. Sometimes they clam up when Cory tries to engage them in conversation. At a recent Monday sales meeting, they slipped sleeping pill powder into Cory's coffee. Obviously, they do not love their neighbor as Jesus commanded.

THE HIGHEST STANDARD

God's love for us sets the standard for our love for Him and others. We learn from John 3:16 that God loved us sacrificially. He gave His Son Jesus for us. On the cross Jesus loved us and gave Himself for us (Galatians 2:20). If we need a picture of true love, all we have to do is look at the cross. Jesus died there for sinners, for those who broke God's commandments and were alienated from Him.

Gypsy Smith, an evangelist of a former generation, preached and discipled others as fervently when he was 75 as he did when he was 25. When someone asked him how he could preach so fervently after decades of ministry, Mr. Smith replied, "I have never lost the wonder of it all."

The apostle John reflected often on the cross of Christ and taught first-century believers to be loyal to the Christ of the cross. Writing in the first New Testament letter that bears his name, John exclaimed, "How great is the love the Father has lavished on us, that we should be called children of God" (1 John 3:1). He wrote those words almost 60 years after standing near Jesus' cross and watching Him die. John never lost the wonder of it all!

Divine love shown so vividly at the cross stirs a reciprocal love in us. As the apostle John observed, "We love because he first loved us" (1 John 4:19). The apostle Paul taught that the Holy Spirit implants "the love of God" in every believer, and he encouraged us to demonstrate that love in all our relationships (Ephesians 5:1).

The apostle Peter urged us to develop love in addition to our faith. He certainly had experienced the self-sacrificing, undeserved love of Jesus. In spite of the fact that

he denied his Lord three times, he received Jesus' unconditional forgiveness and the opportunity to start fresh in
His service (see John 21:15-19).

YOU ARE LOVED

If you have decided to follow Jesus, you are the focus
of His love. He has your best interests at heart and a plan
for your life that holds significance, unspeakable joy, and
lasting peace. Psalm 103 reports that God's love is "as
high as the heavens are above the earth" (verse 11). Even
the most sophisticated technology has not allowed modern science to do more than scratch the surface of space.
How expansive is God's love! Psalm 103:13 compares
God's love to that of a father's "compassion on his children." A loving father wants only what is best for his children. He wants them to succeed and lead a productive,
happy life. He helps his children in any way he can, and he
is available to listen to their questions, needs, and problems. Similarly, believers are invited by their loving heavenly Father to speak to Him any time about the issues they
face, the burdens they bear, and the challenges they confront (Psalm 34:15, 17; Philippians 4:6; Hebrews 4:16).
Our loving heavenly Father also encourages us to commit
ourselves to Him, because He will guide us in His perfect
way (Psalm 37:3-6; Proverbs 3:5, 6; Romans 12:1, 2).

During the War against Terrorism, as in every U.S. military engagement, families were torn apart geographically.
Many members of the U.S. military shipped out for service
in Afghanistan. As Christmas drew near, they sent televised
greetings to family and friends back home. They were sep-

arated by thousands of miles from those who loved them, but they were not separated from their love. Nor are God's children ever separated from His love. Romans 8:38, 39 communicates the apostle Paul's stirring message, "I am convinced that neither death nor life, neither angels nor demons, neither the present nor the future, nor any powers, neither height nor depth, nor anything else in all creation, will be able to separate us from the love of God that is in Christ Jesus our Lord." Furthermore, God's children are never separated from His presence. He promises, "Never will I leave you; never will I forsake you" (Hebrews 13:5).

Animal Rescue found an abandoned Australian shepherd and her three young puppies. The organization was certain it could find a loving home for the mother, but what would happen to the puppies? Each of them had only one eye. Who would choose a one-eyed puppy from an assortment of normal puppies?

The local newspaper of the city where the puppies were rescued ran an article one Friday about the little dogs' plight. It pictured them and announced that the next day they could be seen and adopted at a pet supply store. By noon Saturday, three families welcomed three one-eyed puppies into their homes. Love had saved three little dogs from a perilous fate.

With all due respect to educators and psychologists who emphasize the value of feeling good about oneself and believing in oneself, we must understand that God loved us in spite of our imperfections. Romans 5:8 reports that "God demonstrates his own love for us in this: While we were still sinners, Christ died for us. If it were not for God's inexplicable, undeserved love, we would face a perilous fate.

Knowing how much we owe to divine love, we love the Lord in return by spending time with Him in prayer, reading His Word, and obeying His commands. We must not allow our love to grow cold. Jesus rebuked the church at Ephesus because it had let its love for Him grow cold (Revelation 2:4).

SHARE HIS LOVE

If we truly love the Lord, we will share His love with others. A wife who sincerely loves the Lord will also love her husband and children. A husband who loves the Lord will love his wife and children. Children who love the Lord will love their parents. God's love cannot be contained; it will overflow to our family, friends, neighbors, and those with special needs.

A visit to Niagara Falls, the Honeymoon Capital of the World, allows not only a breathtaking view of the falls but also an insightful view of newlyweds. They are easy to detect. You can see them strolling hand in hand or bundled together in a horse-drawn carriage or exchanging a kiss as they stand at the brink of the falls. However, a trip to Reno may reveal a contrasting view of married life. Unfortunately, sometimes a couple's love may ascend like a rocket but fall like a rock.

CONSIDER THIS SCENARIO:

During the first few months of marriage, Jerry tells his wife Susan, "I think I heard you sniffle, Sweetheart. Perhaps you should make an appointment with the doctor. I wouldn't want you to come down with a cold."

After one year of marriage, Jerry observes, "Honey, I heard you sneeze. After I fix dinner, why don't you go to bed early and get some rest. I'll run out and get some cough syrup for you."

After three years of marriage, Jerry asks, "Will you please use a handkerchief? You don't want to spread germs, do you?"

After five years of marriage, Jerry says, "That sneezing is driving me crazy. Can't you do something about it?"

After ten years of marriage, Jerry complains, "I can't stand another night of your sneezing, hacking, and clearing your throat. If you don't sleep on the sofa, I may have to spend the night in a motel. I have to go to work in the morning, you know!"

Often, a lack of finances threatens a married couple's love for each other. They must guard their love by carefully budgeting and curbing the tendency to live beyond their means. They may have to face the question: Do we love each other more than we love possessions?

Love in a marriage may not survive if either partner shows a greater loyalty to a parent than to his or her spouse. When God instituted marriage, He made it clear that a man must leave father and mother and cleave to his wife (Genesis 2:24). Although the partners ought to love their parents, they must function as a close, loving unit and make their own decisions. They may welcome parental counsel but reject parental interference.

Marriage is sometimes victimized by lack of agreement about child discipline. Mom is too easy on the kids. Dad is too harsh. Or vice versa. However, love for each other and the children will motivate a couple to discuss the issue of discipline, agree on a set of house rules and appropriate disciplinary procedures—and then support each other in implementing the discipline.

An ungodly philosophy of sex may also destroy a marriage. There is no such thing as a harmless affair. Affairs destroy marriages and wreck lives. Even believers can be swept into the tide of immoral behavior by the undertow of movies and TV shows that portray casual sex as fun and normal. The alarming fact that divorce runs higher among Christians than nonChristians raises a red flag. Christians must develop a loving marriage relationship by maintaining a love for God and each other. They must work as hard at keeping their partner as they did in winning their partner; and the words, "I love you," must never fade from marriage.

John and Sarah celebrated their 75th Wedding Anniversary in a nursing home, where they shared a small room but a BIG love before they passed away. While living in the nursing home, they were no longer able to care for themselves, but they still cared for each other. Each tried to make sure the other was comfortable, was eating well, and taking prescribed medicine regularly. Their holding hands and their smiles for each other left no doubt in anyone's thinking that they truly loved each other. If you had met John and Sarah, you would have learned that they had followed Jesus faithfully since childhood. You would have understood that they not only enjoyed Jesus' love but also shared it.

We ought to share Jesus' love outside the home too. Jesus called upon His followers to love their neighbor as themselves. This directive points us to the unfriendly neighbor as well as the friendly one. It includes the unlovely, the forgotten, the abandoned, the hopeless, and the weak, as well as the attractive, the educated, the successful, and the strong. It teaches us to accept others as unconditionally as the Lord has accepted us.

Perhaps you remember a popular song, "What the world needs now is love, sweet love." Followers of Jesus can show the world what real love is. Jesus said, "By this all men will know that you are my disciples, if you love one another" (John 13:35). Such love breaks down the barriers of pride and prejudice. It embraces all people regardless of their color, race, social standing, education, political persuasion, or national origin. As someone observed, pride drew a circle that shut others out. Love drew a wider circle that let them in.

LOVE IN ACTION

If the church wants to make a profound impact on society, it must not simply talk about God's love; it must demonstrate it by reaching out to those in need. The world can be a harsh place. Bombs drop. Jobs get eliminated. Cancer claims loved ones. Terrorism strikes. The economy drops. Bills pile up. Accidents happen. Health fails. Kids rebel. Vandals destroy property. Drive-by shootings take place. Natural disasters jolt us. And sick minds spread hate. In the worst of times believers ought to do their best to share Jesus' love with as many people as possible and use as many means as possible to accomplish our mission. We must refuse to be always learning but never doing. As the apostle James insisted, we must not merely listen to the Word. We must do what it says (James 1:22).

In his book, *In Times Like These*, Dr. Vance Havner offers the following challenge: "The word 'Christian' is both a noun and an adjective. We have too many noun Christians who are not adjective Christians. We need more Christian Christians!" Christian Christians enjoy Jesus' love and also enjoy sharing it with others.

Interactive Discipleship

ANSWER THE FOLLOWING QUESTIONS:

1. Where do you rank love in the pyramid of human needs? Why?

2. What are some negative effects of not being loved by parents and siblings?

3. How does God's love exceed the merits of human love?

4. How might a follower of Jesus appropriately show that he or she loves Jesus?

5. Why does hate operate in the world?

6. Who can you touch today with Jesus' love?

7. How will you show Jesus' love to that person?

8. How might genuine love resolve a marital disagreement over money?

9. How can your church more effectively communicate the message of Jesus' love?

10. Why is genuine love incompatible with prejudice?

READ WHAT THE FOLLOWING PASSAGES SAY ABOUT ENJOYING AND SHARING GOD'S LOVE:

Deuteronomy 7:7-9; Psalm 146; John 3:16—21; 14:21-23; Romans 5:1-8; I Corinthians 13; I John 4:8-19

MAKE DISCIPLES.

- Share this chapter with a friend.
- Tell a friend how you first learned that God loves you.
- Discuss what it means to truly love God and others.
- Send a handwritten note card this week to someone who needs to be encouraged. Draw a heart or smiley face on the card, and write in it: "Jesus loves you and I love you too." Include a small gift with your card.
- Encourage your friend to confront bitterness and seek the Lord's assistance in forgiving others.
- Select one of the Scripture passages cited above, and suggest to your friend that you read it together.
- Pray that you and your friend will be able to forgive others and live free from sin's power.

MULL IT OVER.

Jesus asked Peter, "Do you love me?" How would you answer this question, knowing that Jesus defined love by giving Himself on the cross for you? How can you love Jesus more fully? How will you demonstrate your love for Him this week?

FAITH FOR TODAY AND TOMORROW

Jesus said, "Have faith in God" (Mark 11:22).

What exactly is faith? We hear the word faith spoken often, but most of the time the meaning is up for grabs. "People of faith" is a popular term. "Keep the faith" is another. So is "You gotta have faith!" The concept of faith seems to get squeezed, patted, and pushed into whatever shape people want it to be. But real faith cannot be shaped like play dough to fit our liking. The faith Jesus mentioned in His command has substance, definition, and objectivity. It involves trust—childlike trust—based upon what the Bible teaches, and it focuses on God. Faith without a credible, reliable object is not faith at all. It is presumption or at least misguided and unfounded confidence.

No matter how much faith a man has, he deceives himself if he thinks he can step in front of a freight train without getting injured or killed. That kind of faith is presumption.

A family will go hungry if Mom and Dad refuse to work, believing that angels will drop food, clothing, and money at their doorstep. That kind of faith is presumption.

A college student will fail astrophysics if he believes he doesn't have to study or write assigned papers because God has promised to provide for all his needs. That kind of faith is presumption.

An employee will be shown the door if he believes God will secure his employment while he spends hours on the job reading the Bible and evangelizing fellow employees. That kind of faith is presumption.

So what did Jesus mean when he commanded us to have faith in God? How do we acquire this faith? How does faith impact our lives? Answering these questions correctly will help us follow Jesus faithfully and joyfully.

THE MEANING OF FAITH

The Bible uses the word "faith" in two ways, but each meaning is clearly defined by the context in which "faith" appears. For example, Jude 3 instructs Jesus' followers to "contend for the faith." In the context of Jude's warning that false teaching was invading the Church, "the faith" refers to the body of Truth committed by the Lord to His followers through the inspired Scriptures. Other Scripture passages in which "faith" refers to the Truth include Galatians 1:23; I Timothy 1:18, 19; 4:1, 6; 2 Timothy 4:7; and Jude 20.

The second and more frequent use of "faith" in the

Bible refers to belief or trust. "Have faith in God" means *believe in God—trust in Him.* Hebrews 11 spills over with examples of men and women in Bible times who trusted in God. By faith they "saw" the invisible God, did the impossible, and were invincible. A definition of faith introduces their heroic stories. Verse 1 states that "faith is being sure of what we hope for and certain of what we do not see." The heroes of faith trusted in God so fully that not a single doubt clouded their anticipation of what He had promised. They could not see their eternal rewards, but they held the title deeds to them in their hearts.

Similar trust characterizes those who follow Jesus. We believe that God "exists and that he rewards those who earnestly seek him" (Hebrews 11:6). We cannot see forgiveness, but we believe that God has granted it to us. We cannot see the Holy Spirit, but we know He resides in us. We cannot see heaven, but we anticipate it. We cannot see our treasures there, but we look forward to them. We cannot see Jesus, but we know He is with us, and we gladly obey His commands.

It should not surprise us that those who lack genuine faith question our walk of faith. "How can you believe the Bible? It is an ancient book. It doesn't fit these modern times, we are told. Or we hear people criticize, "Jesus lived 2,000 years ago. Why believe in a dead man?" Occasionally, someone will suggest that Christianity is just a man-made religion. "It may have been okay centuries ago, but it is not relevant now." Faith makes no more sense to our contemporaries than it did to Noah's contemporaries. While he preached, they mocked. But Noah lived to see God do what He had promised, and so will we!

The Bible explains that everlasting life comes only through faith in Him. John 3:36 states clearly and conclusively, "Whoever believes in the son has eternal life." In the first century this truth transformed thousands of lives, including the life of Christianity's most vehement enemy, Saul of Tarsus. Like a fire-breathing dragon, Saul breathed out threats against Jesus' followers, tracked them down, and threw them into prison. However, one day the resurrected Jesus stopped Saul in his tracks. Saul fell to the ground and didn't get up until he acknowledged Jesus as Savior and Lord. Soon Saul became known as the apostle Paul, Jesus' emissary to the Gentile world. Wherever Paul went, he proclaimed salvation through faith in Jesus. He testified: "This righteousness from God comes through faith in Jesus Christ to all who believe. . . . God presented him [Jesus] as a sacrifice of atonement, through faith in his blood. He did this to demonstrate his justice . . . so as to be just and the one who justifies those who have faith in Jesus" (Romans 3:22-26).

When Islam's reputation was besmirched by the terrorist acts of a few Muslims and the abusive rule of Afghanistan's Taliban government, the United States Government and some media personalities appealed to the American people to be tolerant of Islam. They wanted to make the point that Islam is a good religion and one that teaches peace. However, the appeal to be tolerant led many to conclude that Islamic faith is as valid as Christian faith. Followers of Jesus who insisted that He alone is the way to heaven were censured for their exclusive viewpoint. Nevertheless, tolerance and exclusivism can coexist. Christians willingly support the right of Muslims, Jews, Hindus, Buddhists, and others to practice their religion and teach openly, but they believe God grants salvation only to those who trust in His Son Jesus Christ as Savior.

In a television interview a prominent news commentator asked a well-known Christian clergyman if he believed Muslims and Jews would go to heaven. The clergyman replied, "Jesus said 'I am the way and the truth and the life. No one comes to the Father except through me.' So, unless an individual trusts in Jesus Christ, he cannot enter heaven."

"I don't believe that," the commentator retorted. "Jesus preached tolerance and acceptance. So I believe anyone who sincerely follows his religion and lives a good life will end up in heaven. I expect to see a lot of Muslims and Jews there."

Who was right, the commentator or the clergyman? We may even ask who was right, the commentator or Jesus? Don't you agree that Jesus, who never sinned and always spoke the truth, is the reliable authority? The fact is, everyone who trusts in Jesus as Savior will live forever in heaven, but no one will enter heaven who fails to trust in Jesus as Savior. Heaven is not gained by belonging to a religion but by believing on Jesus.

If you were to ask your neighbors and associates how to go to heaven, the majority would probably say something like, "Live a good life." or "Keep the Ten Commandments" or "Observe the Golden Rule." But these answers reveal faith in one's own good works instead of faith in Jesus. Good works cannot qualify anyone for life in heaven. "For it is by grace you have been saved . . . not by works, so that no one can boast" (Ephesians 2:8, 9).

How Do I Acquire Faith?

Faith doesn't come in a pill. Nor is it dispensed as a time-release capsule. We cannot receive it by injection or order it by mail. We do not inherit it from our parents or catch it by hanging out with religious friends. Faith comes by hearing God's Word (Romans 10:17). The better we know God's Word, the stronger our faith can grow.

For example, when we learn from the Bible that Jesus turned water into wine, healed the blind, empowered the lame to walk, cleansed lepers, fed 5,000 with only five loaves and two small fish, calmed a raging storm, and raised the dead, we realize He is Deity and, therefore, all-powerful. As a result, we trust Him to overcome even our most difficult circumstances. When we read in Scripture that God loves us, we trust Him to take care of us. Instead of staying up at night and worrying, we pray and leave our worries with Him. When we read in the Bible that Jesus assigned all authority to the task of making disciples, we believe that we can carry out the assignment successfully. If it were not for the Bible, faith would be groundless and subjective. Every man would be left to himself to decide what to believe.

Elijah, a prophet in Israel in the mid 800s B.C., exercised outstanding faith in the Lord when the nation of Israel had declined spiritually and was worshiping false gods. Here are some episodes from Elijah's life that demonstrate his extraordinary faith:

- In a time of drought and famine, He camped at the Kerith Ravine, east of the Jordan River, drank from the brook there and was fed twice daily by ravens.

- He went to Zarephath and was fed by a widow who was preparing a final meager meal for her son and herself. He promised that her cooking oil and flour would last until the Lord ended the drought.

- He confronted King Ahab in person, even though he knew Ahab considered him the enemy of the state.

Why such faith?

The answer lies in the scenario that surrounded each episode. First, the word of the Lord came to Elijah. Then Elijah did what the Lord told him to do. Finally, he saw that each event turned out as the Lord had promised. Each episode, therefore, strengthened his faith for the next.

Ultimately Elijah's faith was so strong that he confronted hundreds of false prophets in a showdown on Mount Carmel. He challenged them to place an animal sacrifice on an altar and call on their chief god, Baal, to drop fire from heaven to consume it. Then, he told the false prophets he would prepare an animal sacrifice on an altar and call on the Lord, asking Him to drop fire on the sacrifice and consume it. The God who answered with fire would be declared the true God, Elijah proposed.

The challenge was accepted, but the false prophets received no answer to their frantic prayers.

When Elijah took his turn, he drenched his sacrifice with water. Only God could ignite and consume a water-saturated sacrifice—and He did! He did not disappoint Elijah's faith, and the occasion sparked a spiritual renewal in Israel.

Our walk of faith, like Elijah's, includes step-by-step trust in God. He tells us, for example, that He will supply all our needs. Therefore, when we face a crisis of need, we do not panic. Instead, we rely on His promises, and in the nick of time receive what we need. So we take another step of faith when the next crisis emerges. But this time our step is stronger and quicker than before. Experience has taught us convincingly that God keeps His word. The longer we walk with God, the stronger our faith becomes, because God has proven repeatedly that He is worthy our trust.

While sitting in a doctor's waiting room, a Christian teenager thought about the physical examination he would undergo as a college entrance requirement. He was apprehensive about the prospect of attending college 500 miles from home. Also, he was anxious about anticipated college costs. He wondered if he would have sufficient funds to stay in college once he entered it.

Suddenly, an elderly man in the waiting room began to whistle a hymn. The young man recognized it as a hymn frequently sung at church. As the elderly man whistled, the hymn's lyrics danced in teenager's head:

> *"All the way my Savior leads me;*
> *What have I to ask beside?*
> *Can I doubt His tender mercy,*
> *Who through life has been my Guide?*
> *Heav'nly peace, divinest comfort,*
> *Here by faith in Him to dwell!*

For I know, whate'er befall me,
Jesus doeth all things well;
For I know, whate'er befall me,
Jesus doeth all things well."

The testimony of an old man's delight in Jesus' faithfulness to him for many years encouraged the younger believer to entrust his future to Jesus.

HOW DOES FAITH IMPACT OUR LIVES?

Circles in crops attract curiosity seekers who theorize that extraterrestrial aliens carve them in farmers' fields as a means of communicating with earthlings. At least one entrepreneur capitalizes on the presence of such circles in England. Although he attributes their existence to pagans, not aliens, he has attached a mysterious and mystical meaning to them. He leads groups from America to England on investigative research into the religious significance of the circles there, claiming that group members can experience a "religious woo-woo" as they walk the circles. The tour fee runs more than $3,000 per person—enough money to have almost anyone run in circles! As you might expect, no one can define "religious woo-woo."

Unlike faith that thinks a "religious woo-woo" lurks in England's crops, real faith produces real results. Life takes on significance. Daily pressures and trials do not intimidate those who live by genuine faith; they possess a quiet confidence and an eager anticipation of the future.

The first-century Thessalonian believers understood

the value of developing a strong faith. They had abandoned their pagan ways and become Jesus' followers—a decision that riled the overwhelmingly pagan culture that surrounded them. Persecution of the believers was harsh. Nevertheless, the believers persevered by faith. When the apostle Paul greeted them in his first letter, he applauded their active faith (1 Thessalonians 1:3). In his second letter to them, he expressed thanks to God for their faith that was "growing more and more" (2 Thessalonians 1:3).

How had the believers at Thessalonica developed such a strong faith? First Thessalonians 1:6 holds the answer: They had "welcomed the message with joy."

To their credit, they did not hoard the message; they shared it with others. First Thessalonians 1:8 reports their disciple-making effort: "The Lord's message rang out from you not only in Macedonia and Achaia—your faith in God has become known everywhere."

A military highway traversed the city of Thessalonica and ships from many foreign countries docked at its seaport. We can almost see Thessalonian followers of Jesus sharing the message of Jesus with soldiers and sailors. In turn, the soldiers and sailors who became disciples of Jesus carried the message to their respective destinations and perpetuated the disciple-making that had begun in Thessalonica.

Real faith grows from daily Bible reading. As a children's Sunday school chorus teaches: "Read your Bible, pray every day, and you'll grow, grow, grow." However, real faith does not permit us to enrich only our own lives; it motivates us to reach out to others—to be like the Thessalonians. They made disciples in their neighborhoods and community, and they helped to spread Jesus' message worldwide.

"Have faith in God." This is a vital part of the Master's plan for you.

Interactive Discipleship

ANSWER THE FOLLOWING QUESTIONS:

1. How would you define faith?
2. What differences do you see between faith and presumption?
3. How would you respond to someone who claimed that faith is unscientific and therefore invalid?
4. How can you strengthen your faith?
5. How did faith help you face a recent trial?
6. Do you think it is hard to have faith today? Why or why not?
7. How can you set a good example of faith for your own children or for other children you know?
8. How might you encourage a terminally ill person to have faith?
9. What benefits does faith bring to your life?
10. How are faith and disciple-making connected?

READ WHAT THE FOLLOWING PASSAGES SAY ABOUT THE ROLE OF FAITH IN YOUR LIFE:

Matthew 14:22-32; I Thessalonians 1:1-10; 2 Timothy 1:1-7; Hebrews 11; James 2:14-26; I Peter 1:3-9; I John 5:1-5; Jude 17-24

MAKE DISCIPLES.

- Share this chapter with a friend.
- Tell a friend why you believe in Jesus Christ.
- Write a brief poem about faith and deliver it with a plant or plate of cookies to a shut-in.
- Invite a couple of neighbors to your house for refreshments and a brief discussion about the role of faith in family life.
- Agree with a Christian friend to read Hebrews 11 this week and to meet together to share its valuable teachings about faith.
- Select one of the Scripture passages cited above, and suggest to your friend that you read it together.
- Pray that you will meet life's challenges with faith.

MULL IT OVER.

"Have faith in God," Jesus instructed. God is worthy of your trust. He never lies. He cannot fail. His love for you is infinite. His power is unlimited. His plan for you is perfect. His help is always available. And His record is infallible. You can't go wrong if you have faith in God.

PRAYER THAT REACHES HEAVEN

If you play golf or are close to a golfer, you are likely aware of the existence of hundreds of instructional golf videos. Those who take the videos very seriously put their brains on "Replay" when they step up to hit the ball. They recall from one video to bend the knees slightly and balance on the balls of their feet. Remembering another video, they tell themselves they must bring the club head back slowly. Other video instructions flash through their memory: feet, hips, and shoulders must line up with the target; keep left elbow straight; visualize the shot you want to make; cock the wrists; bring the club head down, and sweep through the ball; don't let your hands get ahead of the club; keep your head down; don't fall away from the ball, etc.; ad naseum. With all this material going through a player's head, he may do one or more of the following: (1) go broke buying videos; (2) hit a good shot occasionally—a miracle? (3) take six hours to play 18 holes; (4) lose his golf buddies; (5) forget to hit the ball.

Golf is hard enough without complicating it! Perhaps when it is a player's turn to swing and hit the ball, he should heed Nike's® motto: "Just do it."

That's not a bad motto for prayer either. "Just do it." All the books, sermons, and seminars on prayer accomplish nothing if we don't pray. Furthermore, the Bible does not present prayer as a complicated procedure, but as a simple talk with God.

A group of researchers in Idaho has stepped prayer up to a high level of technology by introducing a computerized prayer amplifier. The "Miracle 6" device is designed to transform the positive desires of prayer into electromagnetic frequencies, which are then directed into six theoretical non-physical dimensions of the universe. Dr. Leonard Horowitz, the device's creator, commented, "Spoken words and/or sacred geometric forms, known throughout the millennia to be associated with miraculous manifestations, are essentially mathematical formulas directing energy inter-dimensionally."

If "Miracle 6" seems too complicated for us, we can always pursue God's simple instruction to "Call to me and I will answer you" (Jeremiah 33:3).

JESUS TAUGHT HIS DISCIPLES TO PRAY

Jesus' disciples didn't always say the wisest things. Occasionally, they submitted selfish requests to Jesus or contradicted what He said or told seekers to scram, but one day they wisely asked Jesus to teach them to pray (Luke 11:1). What might the Church be like today if it showed as much interest in prayer as it shows in prophecy? How many friends and neighbors would become obedient followers of Jesus if we prayed more and programmed less? We certainly subscribe to the power of prayer, but we are much more likely to show up for a church potluck than a prayer service.

In the late nineteenth century a church in a small New England town rang the steeple bell to announce a death. Upon hearing the bell, the townspeople would gather at the church and hear the pastor announce who had died. One day, after weeks of seeing no one attend the mid-week prayer service, the pastor rang the steeple bell. People quickly gathered and asked the customary question, "Who died?"

"No one," the pastor replied. "The church is dead."

Prayer can revitalize a church. As someone wisely observed, "The quickest way to get a church on its feet is to get it on its knees."

Prayer can also revitalize the life of a follower of Jesus and empower him or her for effective living.

Jesus' immediate answer to the disciples' request that He teach them to pray came in the form of what is usually called "the Lord's Prayer"; however, "the Disciples' Prayer" seems to be a more suitable designation.

The prayer Jesus taught His disciples (Luke 11:2-4) can be uttered as a private or public prayer, but it serves best as a model prayer. As such, it has all the essential elements for praying in a manner that pleases our heavenly Father, blesses us, and makes us a blessing to others.

"Father, We Adore You"

Jesus' followers enjoy the privilege of addressing God as "Father." We do not pray to an impersonal, remote, unknown God. He is not the "watchmaker God" deism perceives Him to be—a God who set the world in motion but left it to unwind while He pursues other interests. The title, "Father," endears God to us as the One who loves us, cares about our needs, has our best interests at heart, and wants to spend time with us.

A few human fathers may be dead-beat dads or abusive or unapproachable, but generally fathers are loving, selfless, and willing to do anything in their power to help their children succeed. The love that a devoted father shows to his children mirrors our heavenly Father's love for us.

A father's love was clearly evident on the final hole of The International at Castle Pines Golf Club in early August, 2001. Tom Pernice Jr., winner of the tournament, smiled broadly, as he held his two daughters, Kristen, 7, and Brooke, 6. They had rushed onto the green following Tom's victory. Brooke's hands traced her daddy's smile, giving her the sense of delight her blind eyes could not detect. "There are plenty of golf tournaments, teary-eyed Pernice commented, "but I only have two daughters."

Our loving heavenly Father cherishes His children. He calls them "the apple" of his eye (Zechariah 2:8). Just as we consider the apple (pupil) of the eye extremely precious and worth protecting, even so our Father in heaven considers His children precious and the focus of His protection.

Jesus taught His disciples to pray, "Father, hallowed be your name" (Luke 11:2a). "Hallowed" means to set apart as holy, sacred, and reverent. Although followers of Jesus enjoy an intimate relationship with God, we must not lose sight of how holy and sacred He is. He is not a good buddy in the sky; He is the sovereign Creator of everything. The part of outer space being tapped by our astronauts, telescopes, and satellites is just the outer layer of the vast expanse God has created. His knowledge and power are limitless, and His holy character is flawless. We ought to adore Him with the same kind of praise we read about in Revelation 4:11. All the occupants of heaven fell down before Him, worshiped Him, laid their crowns before Him, and exclaimed: "You are worthy, our Lord and God, to receive glory and honor and power, for you created all things, and by your will they were created and have their being."

No one can deny that God's name does not receive the adoration and reverence it deserves. So many unbelievers—young and old alike— profane His name openly and boldly that it is virtually impossible not to hear them in public places. The jobsite, sports venues, restaurants, malls, and grocery stores are just a few of the places where people take God's name. Doing so has become part of the fabric of society. Movies, television, game videos, music, and print media overflow with such profanity. At times, even believers thoughtlessly exclaim, "My God." They seem to have picked up the expression by osmosis from our post-modern but spiritually primitive culture.

If we sincerely want God's name to be set apart as sacred, holy, and reverent, we can support our prayer, "Hallowed be your name," by representing God well in our daily conduct and relationships. If our lives are holy, those who know us well can perceive that our God is holy. First

Peter I:I5 instructs, "But just as he who called you is holy, so be holy in all you do."

If you were hungry and looking for a good place to eat, how would you choose between two restaurants advertised by two men, each carrying a sandwich board? One sandwich board reads: "Chow down at Charlie's. Delicious meals. Good service. Spotless surroundings." The man carrying Charlie's sandwich board is wearing dirty clothes. His shoes are muddy, his hair is matted, and his beard is stained. The other sandwich board reads: "Dine at Dino's. Superb food. Excellent service. Immaculate surroundings." The man carrying Dino's sandwich board is clean-shaven. His hair is neatly trimmed. His shoes are polished, and his clothes are neat and clean. Wouldn't you eat at Dino's? A clean and neat representative is persuasive. A dirty and untidy representative is not. Representatives of a holy God must be morally clean and holy to be persuasive!

"May Your Kingdom Come"

Jesus taught His disciples to pray, "Your kingdom come." All righteous Jews longed for the promised Messianic kingdom. Its establishment would elevate Israel to a prominent position among the nations. The nation would enjoy the presence of her Savior and King and the tranquility and prosperity that He would bring. Gentile oppression would cease; wars would end; nature would experience productivity and peace; poverty and crime would be only a faint memory; health and happiness would prevail; and worship of the Lord in His holy temple would be restored. (See Isaiah II; 42:I-7; 60; Daniel 7:I4; Micah 4:I-8; Zechariah

8; 14:1-9, 16-21.) The disciples were no exception; they, too, anticipated Messiah's kingdom. On one occasion, two of them asked for leadership positions in the kingdom (Mark 10:35-37). After Jesus' resurrection, the disciples' thinking was riveted on the kingdom. No doubt, they believed the time was right for Jesus to establish His kingdom on earth. They asked, "Lord, are you at this time going to restore the kingdom to Israel?" (Acts 1:6). Jesus' reply did not rule out His establishing the kingdom, but it left the timing of the event in the Father's hands (verse 7).

Bible scholars differ regarding the nature of the kingdom Jesus spoke about. Some believe the kingdom is a future, literal, earthly, messianic kingdom that will last 1,000 years. Others perceive a present spiritual kingdom composed of all believers. They may use the terms "kingdom" and "church" interchangeably. Many of these scholars anticipate a future, literal, earthly messianic kingdom as well. Some, however, believe the kingdom promised by Old Testament Scriptures is entirely spiritual and one that exists today in the hearts of Jesus' followers.

Regardless of the interpretation you prefer, the fact remains that "your kingdom come" is a prayer request for the realization of divine rule over the lives of men and women. As such, it spurs us to make disciples so they can share with us the benevolent rule of the Lord over every aspect of life.

Jesus left no doubt that He wants us to link prayer and disciple-making. He commanded in Luke 10:2, "The harvest is plentiful, but the workers are few. Ask the Lord of the harvest, therefore, to send out workers into his harvest field." But Jesus added an important word to this command. He said, "Go!" (verse 3). The Lord of the harvest has a way of not only pointing out the harvest to us but also of pointing us to the harvest.

Matthew's Gospel adds, "your will be done on earth as it is in heaven," to the words, "your kingdom come." The two requests complement each other. God's kingdom will function in compliance with His will. If we pray sincerely, "your will be done," we will surely incline our own hearts and minds to His will. Having aligned ourselves with the divine will, we will follow Jesus obediently and share His teachings with others.

"GIVE US EACH DAY OUR DAILY BREAD!"

Jesus encouraged His followers to ask God for daily bread. This simple instruction suggests that we can petition God for anything based on need; it is not a *carte blanche* to gain anything based on greed. The apostle John wrote, "This is the confidence we have in approaching God: that if we ask anything according to his will, he hears us. And if we know that he hears us—whatever we ask—we know that we have what we asked of him" (I John 5:14, 15). We learn from the apostle James, however, that we ought to avoid asking for items that we covet. He chided those whose prayers sprang from selfish motives: "When you ask, you do not receive, because you ask with wrong motives, that you may spend what you get on your pleasures" (James 4:3).

Here are a few examples of praying selfishly:

"Lord, please give my mother a daughter-in-law."

"I have always wanted a powerful sports car so I can top 120 miles an hour on the toll road. Any model You choose, Lord, will be okay, but my color choice is fire-engine red."

"Lord, you know how vain my brother-in-law Dave is. He loves to boast about his big, expensive house. Will you please arrange for me to get that top management spot that is open? The salary that goes with the job will allow me to buy a house that will turn Dave green with envy."

"Rev. Mack isn't much of a Bible teacher, but he sure is tall, dark, and handsome. Please guide the congregation to extend a call to him to be our pastor. He would look so good in front of the congregation, and the community would certainly be impressed with his looks."

"Lord, I don't play the lottery very often, but I felt compelled to spend $100 on tickets the other day. Please make me a winner. My wife and I haven't had a really good vacation for ten years. You know we have always wanted to spend a couple of weeks at Waikiki."

Here are a few examples of praying according to God's will and legitimate needs:

"Lord, I am struggling with the cancer diagnosis. Please give me the strength, peace, and determination I need to accept the diagnosis and get on with life. I want others to see that You are the source of my hope and comfort."

"If it please you, Lord, help me find a job so I can provide for my family."

"Lord, help our little girl get over her fear of the dark. Help her to understand that You are watching over her every night and every day."

"Lord, I'm very nervous about dropping off this cake to our new neighbors and inviting them to the neighborhood Bible study. I ask for the courage and wisdom I need to say the right thing. May they see me as a friend."

"Final exams are only two weeks away, Lord. As I

study hard, please help me retain the information I need to pass the exams."

The Scriptures encourage us to depend upon God to supply our needs. King David wrote: "I was young and now I am old, yet I have never seen the righteous forsaken or their children begging bread" (Psalm 37:25). The author of Psalm 84 testified that "no good thing does he [the Lord] withhold from those whose walk is blameless" (verse 11). Jesus taught that we should not worry about our basic human needs, because God cares about us, If we make it our highest priority to seek His kingdom and righteousness, we will never lack what we need. The apostle Paul assured the Philippian believers: "And my God will meet all your needs according to his glorious riches in Christ Jesus" (Philippians 4:19).

In spite of parental opposition, Tim enrolled in Bible college. He believed the Lord wanted him to prepare for the ministry. Because he lacked financial support, he worked 20 hours a week to pay college costs. However, within a couple of weeks of graduating, he received a notice from the college's Accounting Department that his student account showed a $50 debit. The notice also informed him that he would not be allowed to graduate if the balance remained unpaid. Tim's college expenses had eaten his earnings, so what was he to do?

He prayed. Four days before graduation, he received another statement from the Accounting Department. This statement credited his account with $50. He would graduate debt-free.

But where had the $50 come from? Had Accounting made a mistake? Tim went to the Accounting Department and asked about the $50. A clerk explained that an anonymous donor from a neighboring state had sent in the $50 and asked that it be applied to Tim's account. Tim was baffled. He did not know anyone in that state. However, he gladly received the good news as an answer to prayer.

When we ask according to God's will and our legitimate need, we may not know *how* God will answer, but we can be confident that He *will* answer!

CONFESSION

Living in the Western World in modern times makes it difficult to relate to first-century life. We enjoy conveniences people in the first century could not even dream about. We drive cars, talk on cell phones, watch TV, surf the web, operate major appliances, adjust the temperature in our homes by moving a thermostat's indicator, and access cold and hot water with the turn of a faucet. We don't have to visit a public bath. All we have to do is turn on the water in our own bathroom and hop into the tub. First-century people weren't so privileged; if they wanted to soak from head to toe, they had to visit a public bath. By the time they returned home, their feet were dirty. Sandals were no match for the dusty roads.

So what was a person to do upon arriving home and finding that his feet were dirty? Returning to the public bath for another soaking would not make sense. But it made good sense to have a basin of water and a towel at home. Those who owned slaves assigned the foot-washing chore to them.

When Jesus entered the Upper Room with His disciples, He performed the task of a slave by washing His disciples' feet. Also, He used the occasion as an opportunity to demonstrate humility and to teach the need for cleansing from the sins we "pick up" as we walk through an unclean world. He said, "A person who has had a bath needs only to wash his feet" (John 13:10a).

When Jesus' followers sin, they do not need to be washed completely from their sins again, they simply need a partial cleansing. This partial cleansing is what occurs when we pray sincerely, "Forgive us our sins" (Luke 11:4). The apostle John taught, therefore, "If we confess our sins, he is faithful and just and will forgive us our sins and purify us from all unrighteousness" (I John 1:9).

Of course, if we want God to forgive us, we must show forgiveness to others. Jesus taught us to pray, "Forgive us our sins, for we also forgive everyone who sins against us" (Luke 11:4). A forgiving disciple reflects divine forgiveness and therefore makes a powerful statement about the authenticity of his relationship with Jesus.

KEEP ME FROM RISKY SITUATIONS

"And lead us not into temptation," Jesus counseled His disciples to pray. God does not tempt us to do evil, nor does He allow us to endure a trial we cannot overcome in His strength (see I Corinthians 10:13 and James 1:13). However, we can easily find ourselves in situations that expose our breaking point. Our own lusts and weaknesses can drive us into such situations, overwhelm us, and cause us to cave in to sin. These are the kinds of risky situations we need to avoid with the Lord's help.

Some sins may seem less wicked than others, but all sins offend the Lord, hinder our fellowship with Him, and reduce our disciple-making effectiveness. Addiction to pornography or drugs is repugnant, but a hot temper is repugnant too. Armed robbery is criminal, but stealing someone's reputation by employing lies and gossip is criminal too. Both acts violate God's laws. As we pray for protection against risky situations, we can cooperate with the Lord by launching a seek and destroy mission against subtle sins. We can take dead aim against such sins as anger, impurity, hypocrisy, slander, pride, judgmentalism, irritability, unbelief, narrow-mindedness, lukewarmness, resentment, and hate. In other words, if we truly want the Lord to "lead us not into temptation," we will expel sin from our lives no matter what form it takes.

John Paton, the oldest of 11 children born to James and Janet Paton in Dumphries, Scotland, became a missionary to New Hebrides in 1811. His devoted service to Jesus is well documented, but the spiritual influence his father James exerted on him is also well documented. James was a man of prayer. He curtained off a corner of his little house as a prayer closet and went there three times a day to pray. James and his 10 siblings learn to tiptoe past their father's sacred spot.

One can only dream what might happen in our nation if followers of Jesus regularly and devotedly entered a sacred place of prayer at home and included the elements Jesus cited in the model prayer He gave His disciples. Each of us would be changed for the better, and so would the world in which we live and work.

Interactive Discipleship

ANSWER THE FOLLOWING QUESTIONS:

1. Do you think prayer is complicated or simple? Why?

2. How does knowing that God is your Father encourage you to pray?

3. In what ways can you show reverence to God?

4. How do you think most nonChristians perceive God?

5. How do you think most Christians perceive God?

6. How might the life of a follower of Jesus be impacted if he prayed earnestly and sincerely, "Your kingdom come"?

7. What do you want to see happen when you pray, "Your will be done on earth as it is in heaven"? (Matthew 6:10)

8. How might you do God's will today?

9. What needs do you want God to meet today?

10. How can prayer help a follower of Jesus to overcome subtle sins?

READ WHAT THE FOLLOWING PASSAGES SAY ABOUT THE POWER OF PRAYER:

2 Chronicles 7:12-14; Nehemiah 2:1-8; Psalm 5:1-8; Jonah 2; Mark 11:20-26; Acts 12; Ephesians 3:14-21; Philippians 4:6, 7; James 5:13-18

MAKE DISCIPLES.

- Share this chapter with a friend.
- Set a time when you and a fellow believer can pray together.
- Pray specifically for the salvation of a loved one.
- Pray for a political leader. Write a cordial note assuring that leader of your prayers.
- Ask your pastor how you can pray effectively for him, his family, and his ministry.
- Pray daily for the special needs of each member of your family.
- Pray for a neighbor's needs.

MULL IT OVER.

There is a viewless cloistered room
As high as heaven, as fair as day,
Where, though my feet may join the throng,
My soul can enter in and pray.
One hearkening even cannot know
When I have crossed the threshold o'er,
For He alone who hears my prayer
Has heard the shutting of the door.

—Author Unknown

POWER
OVER EVIL

Americans were appalled by the video of Osama bin Ladin gloating over the death and devastation caused by the 9/11/01 terrorist attacks. As a nation, we saw the face of evil and heard evil words by a bloodthirsty religious fanatic! A wolf in sheep's clothing is the most treacherous and ravenous kind of predator. Jesus warned, "Watch out for false prophets. They come to you in sheep's clothing, but inwardly they are ferocious wolves" (Matthew 7:15).

The Bible predicts the rise of a ferocious false prophet in the end times. He is depicted in Revelation 13 as having "two horns like a lamb, but he spoke like a dragon" (verse 11). This wolf in sheep's clothing will deceive millions by "great and miraculous signs" (verse 13) and cause them to worship a powerful political leader. Those who refuse to do so will be targets of extreme persecution (verses 14-17).

The apostle John identified prototypes of the end-times false prophet as having the spirit of antichrist (I John 2:18; 4:1-3; 2 John 7). He warned first-century followers of the true Christ to be on guard against the antichrists.

Like our first-century counterparts, we must guard *our* faith and *the* faith. Often, those who promote false religion project pleasant personalities, employ persuasive tactics, and speak flattering words. We must judge who they are by what they teach. Jesus taught that a bad tree produces bad fruit, whereas a good tree produces good fruit (Mathew 7:17). Evil teaching comes from evil teachers who practice deception.

Evildoers are losers. They cannot dethrone God or destroy truth. Revelation 19:1-21 pulls back the curtain of time and shows us what will happen when Jesus returns to earth. Identified as "Faithful and True," He will strike down all evildoers, including the end-time false prophet and the political ruler he honors, and He will establish His righteous kingdom on earth.

So every follower of Jesus can anticipate the ultimate victory over evil, but can every follower of Jesus overcome evil today? The answer is yes!

OVERCOMING EVIL BEGINS WITH A CHANGED HEART

Cardiologists can diagnose the medical condition of a patient's heart by using such technological wonders as MRI, ultrasound, and angiogram. But only the Great Physician can give us an accurate diagnosis of the spiritual condition of the heart. And only He can restore the heart to spiritual soundness and vitality. According to Jeremiah 17:9, the heart is evil, but the Lord offers a new heart to everyone who repents and trusts in Him. King David understood this truth. He prayed, "Create in me a pure heart, O God" (Psalm 51:10).

The "heart" in biblical terminology represents the source of emotions, thoughts, attitudes, and actions. The heart is evil in the sense that our emotions, thoughts, attitudes, and actions fall far short of the holy standards the Lord has set for us. We may look at the Ten Commandments, for example, and see instantly that we have failed to be what He wants us to be. So much of our behavior is motivated by our selfish wills instead of His sacred will. However, when we believe on Jesus Christ as our Savior, God writes His will on our hearts and puts within them a desire to obey Him (2 Corinthians 3:3; Philippians 2:13).

A songwriter captured the wonder of this profound change of heart with the words, "Things are different now. Something happened to me, when I gave my heart to Jesus." The apostle Paul wrote: "Therefore, if anyone is in Christ, he is a new creation; the old has gone, the new has come" (2 Corinthians 5:17).

When the Lord changes our hearts, He expunges evil and instills righteousness. Ephesians 2:1-3 recalls that we were evil by nature, by choice, and by practice before we believed. Verse 10 underscores what we have become by God's grace, through faith in Jesus: "We are God's workmanship, created in Christ Jesus to do good works, which God prepared in advance for us to do."

What a wonderful change in our lives has been

wrought since Jesus came into our hearts! We have passed from death unto life. We have stepped out of the darkness to walk in the light. We have stopped rebelling against God and have entered into peace with Him. We have escaped from a hopeless end and have embraced an endless hope. We no longer have to fear God's wrath, we live now in the warmth of His love. Evil no longer overcomes us; we overcome evil.

WE OVERCOME EVIL BY RECOGNIZING WHO OWNS US

A bumper sticker asks, "Who owns you?" That's a provocative question that most people might answer by saying, "Nobody owns me. I belong to myself."

But no one is as much his own person as he may think he is. Some people are owned by greed. A passion for money or possessions enslaves them. Others are slaves to an insatiable desire to be popular. Drugs own some people. Sports own those who spend an overwhelming portion of their time, money, and interest on games and collectibles. Even the quest for a PhD can possess a person's life and keep her from enjoying personal and family time.

Now, this may come as a shocker—the Lord owns us believers. First Corinthians 6:19, 20 challenges: "Do you not know that your body is a temple of the Holy Spirit, who is in you, whom you have received from God? You are not your own; you were bought at a price. Therefore honor God with your body."

The apostle Peter echoed Paul's teaching by stating,

"You are . . . "a people belonging to God" (I Peter 2:9). The full force of Peter's words indicates that followers of Jesus are God's property, precisely surveyed, marked, and purchased. If you have purchased property, you can understand this analogy. The purchased property is your possession, and within zoning guidelines and covenants you can do whatever you wish with the property. You can place trees on it, install a lawn, plant flowerbeds, erect a gym set, or build a storage shed. You can design your property according to your plan to serve your heart's desires. Similarly, God has purchased us and has the prerogative to design our lives any way He chooses. His pleasure and glory matter most, but He arranges our lives in a beautiful and peaceful order. As we acknowledge His ownership and submit to His will, we shun evil and pursue righteousness. We confess and forsake wrongdoing and cultivate Christ-like thoughts, attitudes, and deeds. Gradually, our lives— God's property—abounds with the fruit of the Spirit (Galatians 5:22, 23). Impressed with the transformation the Owner has brought to the property He purchased, observers want to meet Him and experience His workmanship firsthand.

WE OVERCOME EVIL BY YIELDING TO THE HOLY SPIRIT'S CONTROL

Having purchased us as His personal property, God has sent the Holy Spirit to each of us. As permanent resident in God's property, the Holy Spirit protects and grooms us to be and do all God wants us to be and do. Our responsibility is to cooperate with Him by yielding ourselves to His control. Romans 6:12-13 instructs: "Therefore do not let sin reign in your mortal body so that you obey its evil desires. Do not offer the parts of your body to sin, as instruments of wickedness, but rather offer yourselves to God, as those who have been brought from death to life; and offer the parts of your body to him as instruments of righteousness."

Scientists have developed amazing robots. Some robots enter dangerous areas and defuse bombs. Some assemble auto parts. Some carry out simple household chores. Some even perform surgical procedures. Of course, they do only what they are programmed to do. Not one robot has its own a mind or emotions. Not a single robot chooses to obey commands because it loves its owner. But Jesus' followers are not robots. We have minds of our own and we possess a wide range of emotions. However, the Holy Spirit uses Scripture to enlighten our minds and fill our hearts with love for Jesus so we gladly obey Him.

WE OVERCOME EVIL BY OBEYING GOD'S WORD

Perhaps you have seen the TV commercial that features parents on Christmas Eve frantically trying to assemble a bicycle for their daughter. Their effort is fraught with uncertainty because instructions were missing from the box containing the bicycle parts. Suddenly awakened by her parents' voices, a young girl leaves her bedroom, peers undetected over the upstairs railing, and listens to their distraught comments. Having assessed the situation, the little girl returns to her bedroom, accesses the bike manufacturer's website, and prints a copy of the instructions. Then she rushes to the upstairs railing and floats the instructions down to a spot near her parents. Not realizing how the instructions turned up, the girl's dad expresses relief, picks up the instructions sheet, and busies himself with the task of assembling the bicycle.

Our heavenly Father has simplified our task of assembling a righteous life. He did not leave us clueless, but provided a clear and complete instruction Book. The Bible serves as our instruction Book. If we read and follow it, our lives will be well constructed—strong and full of good works. If we neglect it, our lives will be dysfunctional. The choice is ours.

Jesus demonstrated the role of Scripture in the battle against evil. The evil one hurled temptation at Jesus when Jesus was physically exhausted after fasting 40 days and 40 nights (Matthew 4:1, 2). He appealed to Jesus to command stones to become bread, to throw Himself down from the highest point of the temple, and to bow down and worship him. But Jesus overcame evil by responding to each temptation with appropriate Scripture. "It is written . . . ," Jesus said.

Theologians debate whether Jesus could have caved in to temptation. After all, He was the perfect, sinless Son of God. Although He was thoroughly human, He did not have a sin nature. Although it seems best to side with those who believe Jesus could not have sinned, we must observe that He resisted temptation by using the Scriptures—the same defense that is available to us. He quoted specifically in order Deuteronomy 8:3; 6:16; and 6:13. The apostle Paul counseled us to "take . . . the sword of the Spirit, which is the word of God" (Ephesians 6:17).

When the devil solicited Jesus to command stones to become bread. He was hoping Jesus would use His divine power selfishly—to satisfy His immediate physical appetite. But Jesus had chosen to live in dependence upon His Father, and He would not use His divine power selfishly. The devil urged Jesus to throw Himself down from the temple's highest point and thereby give angels the opportunity to safeguard Him. The event would serve as a spectacular demonstration of Jesus' prestige. But Jesus had chosen to live humbly as God's obedient servant. He would wait for God to exalt Him at the appointed time. The evil one also showed Jesus all the kingdoms of the world and promised to give them to Jesus if He would worship him. However, what Jesus saw did not lure Him away from loyalty to His Father in heaven. He flatly refused to worship the devil in exchange for the devil's world empire. He would wait for His Father to place earth's kingdoms under His feet (Psalm 2:8, 9; Romans 15:12).

How does Scripture help us cope with inborn desires to be selfish, to be perceived as very important, and to dominate others? It does so by replacing evil desires with holy desires. It rebukes our lusts, corrects our missteps, and directs our paths. Here are several powerful Scripture passages affirming the positive influence of Scripture on our lives:

> "Do not let this Book of the Law depart from your mouth; meditate on it day and night, so that you may be careful to do everything written in it. Then you will be prosperous and successful" (Joshua 1:8).

> "But his delight is in the law of the LORD, and on his law

he meditates day and night. He is like a tree planted by streams of water, which yields its fruit in season and whose leaf does not whither. Whatever he does prospers" (Psalm 1:2, 3).

"How can a young man keep his way pure? By living according to your word. . . . I have hidden your word in my heart that I might not sin against you" (Psalm 119:9, 11).

"I gain understanding from your precepts; therefore I hate every wrong path. Your word is a lamp to my feet and a light to my path" (Psalm 119:104, 105).

"Great peace have they who love your law, and nothing can make them stumble" (Psalm 119:165).

"Sanctify them by the truth; your word is truth" (John 17:17).

"Like newborn babies, crave pure spiritual milk [Scripture], so that by it you may grow up in your salvation" (1 Peter 2:2).

"All Scripture is God-breathed, and is useful for teaching, rebuking, correcting and training in righteousness, so that the man of God may be thoroughly equipped for every good work" (2 Timothy 3:16, 17).

A word of caution: We must do more than read the Bible if we want to overcome evil. We must obey it. Jesus identified as wise "everyone who hears these words of mine and puts them into practice" (Matthew 7:24). Let's suppose a violent storm lay in the flight path of a plane carrying you and other passengers. Who would you like to have as the pilot—someone who ignores all the flight manuals he has read or someone who follows them to the letter? The answer is easy. Staying safe depends upon the pilot's willingness to put into practice what he has learned. Similarly, the follower of Jesus who puts into practice what he learns from Scripture will stay safe when evil threatens to harm him.

Reading and obeying the Bible ought to be as much a habit as brushing our teeth, getting dressed, eating breakfast, and going to work. Each of us needs a Bible reading plan and the discipline to translate what we read into daily life. The assuring promises of the Bible will help us cope with trials, crises, and disappointments. Examples of faith displayed by godly Bible characters will spur us on to trust God when we cannot see what lies ahead. Biblical principles will guide us in our decision-making, and biblical commands will show us what God wants us to do.

Some believers like to read through the entire Bible in a year. If you can devote about 20 minutes per day to reading the best Book of all time, you can read all 66 books of the Bible in a year. Some readers enjoy reading about Bible characters, so they may read about Noah for a few days, then shift to the apostle Peter, proceed to the apostle Paul, jump back to Abraham, move on to David, and focus next on Jesus. Others may choose to read the Bible by studying what it says about doctrine. These readers concentrate on passages or verses that teach about such doctrines as God, Jesus, the Holy Spirit, man, sin, salvation, heaven, hell, future events, justification, sanctification, etc. No matter what Bible study method you follow, you will benefit by keeping a notebook handy or building a computer file to store your findings.

Here are a few items to record in your notebook or computer file:

- your chosen title for the passage of Scripture;
- the passage's theme;
- the key verse;
- major teachings;
- promises;
- commands;
- model prayers;
- examples to imitate;
- failures to avoid;
- principles to live by.

As you read and obey the Bible, you will experience the joy and excitement of following Jesus and becoming a disciple whose life persuades others to follow Him.

WE OVERCOME EVIL BY MAINTAINING CLOSE FELLOWSHIP WITH THE LORD

It's a recurring comment told by a grieving parent to a police officer or judge: "My son (daughter) is a good kid. He (she) just started running around with the wrong crowd." The attempt to shift blame fails to acknowledge that the wayward son or daughter *chose* his or her friends.

Making right choices is essential to a rewarding life at any age. But the most important choice of all concerns our relationship to Jesus Christ. If we choose to follow Him obediently, evil will not overcome us; instead, we will overcome evil. Jesus said, "I am the vine; you are the branches. If a man remains in me, he will bear much fruit" John 15:5). The word "fruit" most likely refers to the fruit of a righteous life, the qualities identified in Galatians 5:22, 23 as "the fruit of the Spirit." Like grapes, these qualities grow in a cluster. They are "love, joy, peace, patience, kindness, goodness, faithfulness, gentleness, and self-control."

Vinedressers in Jesus' time knew that low, sagging branches did not produce quality clusters of grapes. Grapes hanging from low branches usually touched the ground and rotted or they failed to mature because they did not get enough sunlight. The vinedressers, therefore, pulled the low branches away from the soil and tied them up higher on the vine, where they would enjoy more sunlight. Jesus understood that the closer His followers are to Him, the Vine, the more productive we are.

Staying close to Jesus is the best way to live. If we find that we are not as close to Him as we once were, we need not wonder who moved. Jesus never leaves or forsakes His followers, but occasionally we wander like dumb sheep. However, we can stay close to Him always and overcome evil if we take time every day to read the Bible and pray, depend upon Him to guide us throughout each day, count our blessings and thank Him for them, confess and forsake our sins, and stay focused on the task of introducing others to Him.

Survivalists caution that getting lost in mountainous terrain in wintertime can be deadly. They advise staying awake and active. Falling asleep, they warn, could cost a disoriented hiker his life. Similar advice is appropriate for all who follow Jesus Christ in a world that evil has turned cold and dangerous. We dare not give in or give up because evil surrounds us. We dare not succumb to the temptation to lower our standards and drop our guard. Evil is a deadly foe, but it is not invincible. Through Christ, we are invincible (Romans 8:37). Let us, therefore, stay alert and actively make disciples. Darkness cannot prevail where lights shine brightly.

Interactive Discipleship

ANSWER THE FOLLOWING QUESTIONS:

1. Why is evil so pervasive in spite of education, affluence, and technology?

2. What evil deceptions have you witnessed?

3. Why is religious deception especially dangerous?

4. How do you know evil will experience a decisive defeat?

5. What might you do to combat evil in your community?

6. Who owns you? How does your life style show who owns you?

7. How can you cooperate with the Holy Spirit as He develops Christlike qualities in you?

8. What sins seem most persistent in your life? What actions will you take today to overcome them?

9. How does the Bible help Jesus' followers over-come evil?

10. What Bible-reading plan will you implement to-day?

READ WHAT THE FOLLOWING PASSAGES SAY ABOUT OVERCOMING EVIL:

Psalm 37:7-20; Proverbs 16:5-8; Matthew 4:1-11; 24:36-51; John 3:16-21; Romans 6:1-23; Ephesians 2:1-10; 5:1-14; I Timothy 6:11-16; I John 2:12-17

MAKE DISCIPLES.

- Share this chapter with a friend.
- Agree with your spouse or a friend to read the Book of Philippians in two days.
- Meet with your reading partner to discuss the main teachings you found in Philippians, and share how these teachings helped you overcome evil.
- Keep a daily record this week of the temptations you faced and how the Lord helped you overcome them. Share your notes with a friend if you would feel com-fortable doing so. Or ask a friend how you can help each other resist temptation.

MULL IT OVER.

Vice is a monster of such frightful mien,
As to be hated needs but to be seen'

Yet seen too oft, familiar with her face,
We first endure, then pity, then embrace.

—ÅLEXANDER POPE

Perhaps one of the greatest evils today is the evil of becoming desensitized to evil. It is easy to grow accustomed to evil because images of evil enter our homes daily through TV. Our newspapers report inhumane treatment and crimes, and our radio talk shows and news reports spill over with information that bombards our sensibilities. After a while, evil no longer shocks us. But it should, and it should shake us and spring us into action. What might happen to evil if every follower of Jesus were to commit to making at least one disciple a month?

JOY THAT JUST WON'T QUIT

Sixteen-month-old Jasmine was kidnapped from her mother at a Chicago Greyhound Bus station by a woman pretending to be a Good Samaritan. It happened just four days before Christmas, but the story ended happily a couple of days later. Jasmine was found in West Virginia and returned to her mother, who hugged her child and exclaimed that she was "overwhelmed with joy."

Jesus told three stories that illustrate the immense joy that surrounds the return of a lost soul to God. The Story of the Lost Sheep tells how a shepherd left 99 sheep to rescue one lost sheep. When he found it, he joyfully hoisted it onto his shoulders, carried it home, and summoned his friends and neighbors to rejoice with him (Luke 15:4-7). The Story of the Lost Coin features a woman's thorough search of her home for a lost coin. When she found it, she invited her friends and neighbors to rejoice with her (verses 8-10). The Story of the Lost Son reports the homecoming of a rebellious, wayward son. His father ran to meet him, gave him a big bear hug, outfitted him with new clothes and a ring, and hosted a festive meal to celebrate his return (verses 11-24).

Joy fills not only heaven when a lost person and the heavenly Father are reunited but also the heart of the person returning to the Father. Do you remember what happened when you became God's reclaimed son or daughter and a follower of Jesus? You experienced great joy because you knew God had forgiven you and granted you eternal life. You no longer wondered where you would spend eternity; you knew you would live forever in heaven. Life took on eternal significance. Every subsequent day provided fresh opportunities to fellowship with Jesus and represent Him to relatives, friends, neighbors, and associates. You can share the prophet Isaiah's joy. He exulted: "I delight greatly in the LORD, my soul rejoices in my God. For he has clothed me with garments of salvation and arrayed me in a robe of righteousness" (Isaiah 61:10). You can identify with the Thessalonians who "welcomed the message [the message about Jesus] with the joy given by the Holy Spirit" (1 Thessalonians 1:6).

But can joy last? Will it stick when trouble strikes? Will it be there when the vitality of youth vanishes and the ravages of old age arrive? Can it survive unexpected bad news? If you don't have a dime in your pocket, will you still have joy in your heart?

JOY FOR ALL SEASONS

Jesus promised that His joy would remain in us and be complete if we meet certain conditions. But before we examine the conditions, we ought to think about the kind of joy He pledged. He called it " my joy." He used the same words when He prayed to His Father and said, "I am coming to you now, but I say these things while I am still in the world, so that they [Jesus' followers] may have the full measure of my joy within them" (John 17:13). Jesus' joy far exceeds happiness. Being happy depends on favorable circumstances, but joy remains intact and strong even in horrendous circumstances. Isaiah described Jesus correctly as "a man of sorrows" (Isaiah 53:3). Jesus wept at the tomb of Lazarus. He wept outside Jerusalem because that ancient "holy" capital rejected Him. In the Garden of Gethsemane, just prior to His arrest, He told Peter, James, and John, "My soul is overwhelmed with sorrow to the point of death" (Mark 14:34). Yet, Jesus never lost the joy of living in unbroken fellowship with His Father and in perfect compliance with His will. He endured even the cross "for the joy set before him" (Hebrews 12:2).

Jesus proved that joy and fun are not Siamese twins. Joy can exist even when fun is absent. Having fun depends upon happy occasions, whereas having joy depends upon a close relationship with Jesus. Fun occurs when the good times roll, but joy abides in the worst of times as well as in the best of times. Joyful people can have fun, but people who have fun may not have joy. Those who conform to the ways of the world may have fun, but only those who conform to the will of God have real joy. Fun is temporary. Joy is eternal. Fun is manmade, but joy comes from God. Joy is neither physical nor material; it is supernatural and spiritual. A songwriter gave accurate directions for finding joy. He wrote: "If you want joy, real joy, wonderful joy, let Jesus come into your heart." Perhaps it is time the church stopped asking, "Are we having fun yet?" and starting asking, "Do we have Jesus' joy yet?"

Having Jesus' joy through thick and thin, in the storms of life as well as in the sunshine, in loss as well as gain, in sadness as well as gladness, in hurt as well as health, we must pursue a biblical life style.

JOY AND OBEDIENCE ARE INSEPARABLE

Obedience is a key characteristic of a biblical life style. Jesus said, "Now remain in my love. If you obey my commands, you will remain in my love, just as I have obeyed my Father's commands and remain in his love. I have told you this so that my joy may be in you and that your joy may be complete" (John 15:10, 11). Based on Jesus' words, we can see it is possible to experience hard times and joy simultaneously but impossible to be joyful and disobedient simultaneously.

So the million-dollar question is, What has Jesus commanded us to do? A search of the Gospels uncovers His commands, but His will for us is revealed in the entire Bible. Here are a number of commands we can use as a brief test of our obedience to Jesus:

- "Let your light shine before men" (Matthew 5:16).

- "Love your enemies and pray for those who persecute you" (Matthew 5:44).

- "Store up for yourselves treasures in heaven" (Matthew 6:20).

- "Do not worry" (Matthew 6:25).

- "Follow me" (Matthew 8:22).

- "Ask the Lord of the harvest . . . to send out workers into his harvest field" (Matthew 9:38).

- "Take my yoke upon you and learn from me" (Matthew 11:29).

- "Give to Caesar what is Caesar's, and to God what is God's" (Matthew 22:21).

- "Love the Lord your God with all your heart and with all your soul and with all your mind. . . . Love your neighbor as yourself" (Matthew 22:37-39).

- "Watch out that no one deceives you" (Matthew 24:4).

- "Go and make disciples of all nations, baptizing them in the name of the Father and of the Son and of the Holy Spirit, and teaching them to obey everything I have commanded you" (Matthew 28:19, 20).

- "Repent and believe the good news" (Mark 1:15).

- "If anyone would come after me, he must deny himself and take up his cross daily and follow me" (Luke 9:23).

- "Love one another" (John 13:34).

- "Do not let your hearts be troubled. Trust in God, trust also in me" (John 14:1).

- "Remain in me" (John 15:4).

- "Remain in my love" (John 15:9).
- "Ask and you will receive" (John 16:24).

Tests aren't always pleasant, are they? Sometimes they reveal our flaws, but when we pass, we are elated. Do you remember studying hard to pass an Algebra test? If you are like most people, learning Algebra was about as much fun as a root canal. When you took the final Algebra test, you may have lost five pounds by perspiring heavily. But when you discovered later that you had passed the test, you experienced incredible joy. The passing grade was worth all the effort. Similarly, you studied hard to earn a driver's license. Yes, you were nervous when you took the written test and nearly in shock when you took the road test, but when the examiner announced you had passed, you felt like you were floating on Cloud Nine. As you read the preceding abbreviated list of Jesus' commands, did you find yourself passing or failing the test of obedience to Jesus? Do you need to revisit some of Jesus' commands and retake the test? A life of joy is the reward for passing, and that's a whole lot better than passing even an Algebra test or a driving test.

PRAYER TURNS THE KEY THAT UNLOCKS THE DOOR TO JOY

Soon after His resurrection, Jesus joined two disciples in their journey from Jerusalem to Emmaus. The disciples were kept from recognizing Jesus as they walked the seven-mile stretch, but the four hours of conversation with Jesus was memorable and highly instructive. When they reached Emmaus, the two disciples invited Jesus into their home.

There, at the evening meal, they perceived that their guest was Jesus, but Jesus quickly disappeared. They asked each other, "Were not our hearts burning within us while he talked with us on the road and opened the Scriptures to us?" Obviously, their fellowship with Jesus had filled their hearts with great joy. Talking with Jesus has a way of doing that!

Jesus encouraged us to pray and promised that our prayers would be answered and our joy would be complete if we asked Him for anything in His name (John 14:13, 14; 16:23). Prayer, then, is the key that unlocks the door to joy. But what does it mean to pray in Jesus' name?

It doesn't mean we should attach Jesus' name to the end of our prayers as a magical mantra, a kind of *abracadabra*, *Shazaam* or *Open Sesame*. Closing each prayer with the words, "in Jesus' name," can be meaningful, but only if we understand what it means to ask in Jesus' name. It means to ask as His representative for whatever will further His work and bring glory to Him.

Let's compare prayer to a company credit card. A sales rep may enjoy the privilege and benefits of a company credit card if he uses the card to achieve his company's mission. He might legitimately use it for a sales visit from his Chicago base to a West Coast city if the trip would benefit the company he represents. He could use his card to purchase round-trip airline tickets, rent a car, charge his meals, and entertain clients—all in the name of his company. Let's assume, though, that during the business trip he uses the company credit card to purchase a set of golf clubs, a dozen golf balls, a pair of golf shoes, and a golf shirt. We would call those purchases unauthorized uses of the credit card, because they are self-serving and do not advance the mission of the company that granted the card. Similarly, Jesus granted a *carte blanche* to His followers authorizing us to acquire anything we ask for in His name. However, to receive what we ask for we must pray according to His will, to advance His cause, and to enhance His reputation on earth.

A follower of Jesus might legitimately pray for a set of golf clubs, a dozen golf balls, a pair of golf shoes, and a golf shirt, but she would need to ascertain that receiving these items would further the Lord's cause and enhance His glory. Most of us would find it difficult to understand how asking for golf equipment and golf wear would be up to par with the Lord's will, but they might be in certain situations. The issue is not what we ask for (Jesus invited us to ask for anything) but our motive for asking. If our motive is pure, the results are always consistent: answered prayer and complete joy.

SIN STEALS OUR JOY

If we obey Jesus, we experience His joy, but if we disobey Him, we forfeit His joy. Bob and Tina discovered this truth. Early in their married life, they faithfully taught Sunday school, gave cheerfully to the Lord's work, read the Bible, prayed, told their acquaintances tactfully but candidly that they were believers, demonstrated a righteous life style, and endeavored to make disciples. Their shared joy was abundant and evident. Everything began to change, though, when Bob took a new job in a distant city. They kept looking for a church just like the one they had left, but they never found it. Their church attendance became irregular, then it ceased altogether. They gravitated to new friends with a materialistic, self-centered approach to life. Before long, they were making the rounds of cocktail parties and upscale bars. They made expensive purchases, hoping to impress their friends. Bob began to spend long hours at the office, hoping to get noticed and advanced. Tina resented his absences, and became sullen and withdrawn. Bob tired of coming home to an irritable wife, so some nights he stayed at a hotel downtown. The two had left a joyful marriage and were sliding into a divorce as surely as skiers trapped in an avalanche cascade to a snowy grave. Feeling desperate, they called a pastor and set an appointment for counseling.

After listening carefully to Mark and Tina's story, Pastor J observed: "Mark, Tina, somewhere along the way you slipped away from following the Lord and began following the crowd. When you did so, you began to lose not only your sense of direction but also your joy. You are not the first to have made such a tragic mistake."

Lifting a Bible from his desk, Pastor J opened it to Psalm 51. "Israel's King David was joyful when he obeyed the Lord. Once he was so joyful that he danced in front of the Ark of the Covenant. Later, however, he fell eyes-first into sin. He committed adultery, and that sin stole his joy. He became miserable, and his personal world was caving in. Finally, he confessed his sin to the Lord. Psalm 51 records his confession. Let me read just verses 12 and 13 of Psalm 51. 'Restore to me the joy of your salvation and grant me a willing spirit, to sustain me. Then will I teach transgressors your ways, and sinners will turn back to you.' Mark and Tina, don't you think you need to offer your confession to the Lord, turn from your wayward life style, and make obeying Jesus your number one priority? If you will do so, the Lord will restore your joy and use you again to turn others to Him."

Mark and Tina glanced at each other through tear-filled eyes, grasped hands, and bowed their heads. In their hearts they had resolved to return to a life of obedience and joy.

WORSHIP KEEPS THE JOY FRESH

Worshipers crowd a temple in India, where they revere and give offerings of food to the gods who live there. Of course, nonChristian temple worship takes place around the world, but the big shocker in this case is *the gods are rats.* Hordes of rats scurry, scratch, and sniff among the worshipers, oblivious to the sacred place they hold in the worshipers' esteem. If you can picture any joy in worshiping rats, your imagination rivals that of the creators of Fantasia!

But you don't have to have an active imagination to picture the joy the disciples experienced when they worshiped the risen Son of God. Luke 24:51, 52 reports that they worshiped Him as He blessed them and ascended to heaven. Then they "returned to Jerusalem with great joy."

There is no joy in worshiping a dead savior. The apostle Paul commented in I Corinthians 15 that our "faith is futile" if Christ did not rise from the dead and "we are to be pitied more than all men" (verse 17, 19). But he quickly added, "But Christ has indeed been raised from the dead" (verse 20).

Because Jesus arose from the dead, we worship Someone who guarantees us eternal life. "Because I live, you also will live," He promised in John 14:19. The prospect of living forever sustains our joy.

Because Jesus arose from the dead, we worship Someone who possesses all power in heaven and on earth (Matthew 28:18). We can carry out our assignment of making disciples, knowing that He is fully in charge and capable of granting success. Joy floods our hearts as we contemplate His unlimited authority and worship Him.

Because Jesus arose from the dead, we worship Him as the living Friend who hears every prayer we utter (Hebrews 4:14-16). We revere Him and praise Him for His availability and benevolence. And joy warms our souls as we do so.

Because Jesus arose from the dead, He serves as our defense attorney in the presence of our heavenly Father (I John 2:1). When we sin, He represents our interests before the Judge of all the earth. He points to His sacrifice on the cross as the full satisfaction of the penalty for our sins. As we worship the Lord, we rejoice in His ministry in Heaven on our behalf.

JOY ACCOMPANIES THE WORK OF MAKING DISCIPLES

Bible scholars seem to agree that the apostle Paul was the most effective disciple-maker in history. His witness for Jesus Christ stretched from Jerusalem to Rome, from Judea to Asia and Europe, and from marketplaces to the halls of Roman justice. Wherever he went, he shared the good news about Jesus' love and forgiveness. Many Jews and Gentiles believed, causing great rejoicing in heaven and in Paul's heart as well. He fondly referred to those whom he had introduced to Jesus as his "joy" (Philippians 4:1; I Thessalonians 2:19, 20).

Making money might make us rich, but making disciples will definitely make us joyful. The psalmist promised, "He who goes out weeping, carrying seed to sow, will return with songs of joy, carrying sheaves with him" (Psalm 126:6). If we invest part of our income wisely, we may be glad someday; but if we invest our lives wisely in the work of making disciples, we will rejoice now and forever. Whatever buildings we construct will eventually fall, but the lives we help to build on Jesus, the Rock of Ages, will stand firm eternally.

Evangelist Dwight L. Moody recalled seeing a painting in a Chicago art gallery that he felt was the most beautiful painting he had ever seen. Entitled "Rock of Ages," it depicted a person clinging with both hands to a cross on a rock in a stormy sea. Later, he saw a similar painting, but this one featured a person clinging to the cross with one hand and reaching down with the other to rescue someone from the churning sea. Moody commented that the second painting surpassed the beauty and significance of the first. Nothing in all of life surpasses the beauty, significance, and joy of making even one disciple! No wonder King Solomon wrote, "He who wins souls is wise" (Proverbs 11:30).

JOY AND HOPE ARE PARTNERS

Pity the person who has no hope of living blissfully beyond the grave, whose only hope is to live happily and die with dignity. Such an inferior hope is often unfulfilled and is never accompanied by joy. But the hope Jesus' followers treasure will definitely be fulfilled and is always accompanied by joy. Romans 5:2 affirms that believers "rejoice in the hope of the glory of God." The apostle Peter referred to this hope as a living hope and credited it with filling us "with an inexpressible and glorious joy" (I Peter 1:3, 8). Hebrews 6:19 describes this hope as "an anchor for the soul, firm and secure." There is nothing indefinite about our hope. It is ironclad, indestructible, steady, and imbedded in God's promises.

Our hope fills us with joy because we foresee a bright future, an eternal home, and a face-to-face relationship with our Lord and Savior. Sin, sickness, sorrow, crime, callousness, clamor, regrets, resentment, rebellion, uprisings, unfairness, unhappiness, disappointments, disasters, and dictatorships will have ended. Heaven holds only what makes us joyful and grateful for who God is and what His grace has accomplished. If you feel like shouting hallelujah, your hope and joy are in good condition.

A woman on a passenger ship off the coast of Newfoundland asked a crewmember, "Is it always foggy on the banks of Newfoundland?"

"I don't know, Ma'am," he replied. "I don't live there."

Jesus said we are in the world but not of the world but He has sent us into the world as His disciples (John 17:16, 18). A fog of fear, despair, and uncertainty blankets the world, but we don't live in the fog. Jesus has lifted us above fear, despair, and uncertainty. He has given us a clear vision of His purpose for our lives, and His joy abounds in us. Perhaps the brightness of His joy will burst through the fog and cheer many who live there.

Interactive Discipleship

ANSWER THE FOLLOWING QUESTIONS:

1. What do you see as the major differences between happiness and joy? fun and joy?

2. Have you experienced joy in the thick of a hard trial? To what do you attribute that joy?

3. How could Jesus, "a man of sorrows," promise joy to His followers?

4. How can you increase heaven's joy?

5. Can a person who seldom prays have abiding joy? Explain.

6. If you had to choose between prosperity and joy, which would you choose? Why?

7. What, if anything, have you prayed for recently that sprang from a selfish motive? What resulted?

8. What, if anything, have you prayed for recently that sprang from a pure motive? What resulted?

9. How can you share your joy with family members? associates? neighbors?

10. What features of heaven do you anticipate joyfully?

READ WHAT THE FOLLOWING PASSAGES SAY ABOUT JOY:

Psalms 16; 126; Isaiah 12:1-6; Luke 1:42-55; 15:11-

24; 2 Corinthians 8:1-7; Philippians 4:1-4; Hebrews 10:32-39; I Peter 4:7-13

MAKE DISCIPLES.

- Share this chapter with a friend.
- Spark a conversation with a neighbor concerning the challenge of being joyful in spite of alarming world conditions. Share that you depend upon Jesus for your joy.
- Send a cheerful card or note to someone who may be discouraged. Include a verse of Scripture that mentions joy.
- Spend at least five minutes in prayer, praising the Lord for what brings you joy.

MULL IT OVER.

Jesus never fails His followers. He is with us all the time. He hears our prayers, carries our burdens, calms our sorrows, and equips us for service. He died to save us, lives to keep us, and is preparing a place in heaven for us. How can we be anything but joyful?

WORDS
TO
LIVE BY

We, the people . . . . So begins the Preamble to the Constitution of the United States. These words, introduced more than two and a quarter centuries ago, have been cherished by generations of Americans. They give us a sense of destiny and political direction. But the words of the Bible are to be cherished and implemented even more than history's most inspiring political words. The words of the Bible are, after all, God's words. They prepare us not only for daily life but also for eternal life. They comfort us, cheer us, and challenge us. They provide clarity for our thinking, conviction for our beliefs, confidence for our faith, certainty for our hope, and courage for our way of life. God's words are true, timeless, and trustworthy, rich, rewarding, and relevant.

The Old Testament predicted Jesus' life on the

earth, the Gospels depict His life on the earth, and the rest of the New Testament joins the Old Testament and Jesus' teachings in guiding us into a life that reflects Jesus' presence in us as we live on the earth. When Jesus walked among men and women, He affirmed the Old Testament by quoting from it often as the supreme authority for faith and life. His own teachings, He said, "are spirit and they are life" (John 6:63). He promised that a life built on His words would be indestructible (Matthew 7:24, 25). Further, He predicted the flawless writing of the New Testament when He told His disciples the Holy Spirit would guide them into all truth (John 16:13). Attesting to the fact that the Bible is the product of divine inspiration, the apostle Paul declared that "all scripture is God-breathed" (2 Timothy 3:16). We cannot fail if we live by the words God has made available to us in the Bible.

Thousands of books would not provide adequate space to comment on all the words the Bible gives us to live by, so let's confine our thinking to just a few of the many words Jesus spoke. They will serve us well as life principles.

FOLLOW ME

Aren't you glad Jesus spoke plainly? He used simple words to communicate profound truths and make His will known. When He stepped into the lives of those who would become His disciples, He did not say, "I have decreed that you neither vacillate from nor circumambulate my prescribed pedagogy, epistemics, demeanor, and modus operandi." He said simply, "Come, follow me" (Matthew 4:19).

We can easily understand what it means to follow. When we were children, we played a game called "Follow the Leader." The instructions were simple: Go wherever the leader goes, and do whatever the leader does. The instructions for following Jesus are the same: Go wherever Jesus goes and do whatever Jesus does.

Where did Jesus lead His disciples after inviting them to follow Him? He led them to the destitute and dying, the sick and lonely, to sinners, to the rejected, to the lost people of Israel, and to those who lived outside the fold of Israel. He led them to people who needed to know about God's love and forgiveness, people who needed to be reconciled to God, people who needed to experience God's peace and understand His purpose for their lives.

Jesus still leads His disciples—you and me and all our fellow believers—to share His love and teachings with needy people. Some live in suburbia, some live on inner-city streets, others live in rural villages, and some live on your street, but all live in a state of unrest, deep concern, and unsettling confusion about life. Whether a needy person's home is a fancy "castle" on a wooded lot or a flimsy cardboard box under a bridge, he needs to learn that Jesus offers forgiveness and the opportunity to become a member of God's forever family.

And what did Jesus do on earth? What does He want each of His followers to do? He always did what pleased His Father in heaven (John 8:29). He made disciples, particularly 12 men, whom He trained for the ongoing work of making disciples. He prayed in all kinds of circumstances. He triumphed over temptation (Hebrews 4:15). He patiently endured harsh trials (5:7, 8; I Peter 4:1). He ministered faithfully (Mark 10:45), and He fulfilled His Father's will (John 17:4). Following Jesus, then, involves making disciples, praying, being patient, persevering, and performing God's will.

Following Jesus is a personal responsibility. Each of us is directly accountable to the Lord for how closely we follow Him. We should not lag behind Him because we think others are not following Him closely. Nor should we question the load He gives us to carry. Even if the load seems heavier than what others are carrying, we should not complain.

During a seaside stroll, Jesus told Peter what lay in store. Peter would tend and feed Jesus' sheep and lambs and die as a martyr in his old age. Seeing that John was walking behind them, Peter asked, "Lord, what about him?" (John 21:21).

"If I want him to remain alive until I return, what is that to you? You must follow me," Jesus replied (verse 22).

It isn't hard to throw a pity party for ourselves, is it? Usually the party is preceded by such thoughts as

Why do I have to be the one to give up so many of my Saturdays to fix what's broken at church?

No one else is willing to teach the Middle School Sunday school class. So why should I bother?

Here I am in the church's kitchen, cooking another dinner for the Women's Missionary Union. A younger woman should do this work.

How come the pastor calls on me for service at the downtown mission? I never see Frank, Melissa, Jodi, or Miguel show up for mission ministry.

But pity parties can and should be replaced with praise parties. Praise parties are preceded by such thoughts as

It's such an honor to be one of Jesus' followers.
Jesus always leads me in the right way.
Jesus never asks me to go where His grace doesn't reach.
I wish everyone could experience the joy of following Jesus.
All Jesus asks me to do is obey Him. I can handle that.
Jesus has promised He will never leave me or forsake.
It's wonderful to share Jesus' love with others.

What might each new day bring if each of us started it with Jesus' words, "Follow me," engraved in our thinking?

LET YOUR LIGHT SHINE

Can you picture what life would be like if suddenly every trace of light disappeared? Finding ourselves in total darkness, we would stumble about and wander aimlessly. The risk of injuring ourselves would be high, our anxiety would escalate, and life would seem extremely dull and empty. Light from the sun warms us and nudges flowers into beautiful exhibits of divine creation. It soaks up drabness from the earth and replaces it with exciting splashes of color. It serves as a source of power and even brightens our outlook on life. Lesser forms of light illuminate our homes, assist our vision, and guide our steps.

Can you picture the kind of dark world Jesus entered two millennia ago? Spiritual darkness engulfed our planet. Israel, God's chosen nation, had not received a word from Him in 400 years. Not a single prophet had communicated a message from God. Not a scrap of Scripture had been written. The pagan Roman Empire had put a stranglehold on Palestine, the Promised Land. The Jews languished under Roman rule, and they received no spiritual help from their religious leaders, the Pharisees and scribes. Those religious leaders amounted to blind guides escorting their followers into a ditch. The only rays of light emanated from a few righteous Jews, who were hoping their Messiah would come, and from a scrappy religious maverick named John. John was calling upon the Jewish nation to repent and prepare for the Messiah's arrival.

Then Jesus, the virgin-born Son of God and chief descendant of Israel's King David, presented Himself to the Jews! He identified Himself as "the light of the world," and promised, "Whoever follows me will never walk in darkness, but will have the light of life" (John 8:12). Although the nation rejected the Light and tried to snuff it out at the cross, some men and women believed on Jesus as the Messiah and became His followers. They stepped out of spiritual darkness and into the light. Their sins fell away. Righteousness, peace, joy, hope, and a sense of purpose and direction filled their hearts and minds. They became light-bearers.

We, too, have stepped out of spiritual darkness and into the light by faith in Jesus Christ. A cloud of darkness no longer hangs over our minds and blankets it from the truth. We understand now what the apostle Paul meant when he wrote. "The god of this age [Satan] has blinded the minds of unbelievers, so that they cannot see the light of the gospel of the glory of Christ, who is the image of God" (2 Corinthians 4:4). We no longer walk in darkness; we have the light of life!

Privilege begets responsibility, though. The light is not ours to hoard but to hold out to others. We must share it, not shield it. Jesus said, "Let your light shine before men, that they may see your good deeds and praise your Father in heaven" (Matthew 5:16). Can there be any doubt that the present world needs our light? Technology is at an all-time high, but true spirituality is at an all-time low. The occult fascinates our society. Books and movies about witches and wizards draw readers and viewers as a magnet draws iron filings. Simple questions about the Bible posed to educated contestants on TV shows are met with silence or answers that are as far removed from accuracy as Jupiter is from Earth. Moses did not write one of the four Gospels, nor did he lead animals onto the ark. Jeremiah was not one of the 12 disciples. And John the Baptist did not baptize in the Nile River. Although biblical teachings helped forge America's freedom and frame its Constitution, they are considered by many today to be too rigid and exclusive for the popular pluralistic mindset. We are advised by liberal thinkers to celebrate diversity, but our Christian beliefs aren't welcome at the celebration.

In his book, *John Adams*, David McCullough writes about Harvard in 1755: " 'All scholars,' it was stated in the college rules, were to 'behave themselves blamelessly, leading sober, righteous, and godly lives.' There was to be no 'leaning' at prayers, no lying, no blasphemy, fornication, drunkenness, or picking locks" (*John Adams*, Simon & Schuster, New York, 2001, p. 36). One cannot imagine a modern American university publishing such rules and risking ridicule at best, censure, lawsuits, and even closure.

It is much safer for a university to scoff at Christian values than to support them and to deny absolute truth than to demand it of its faculty and students.

How can we beam the light into a dark culture? Getting irate and storming the citadels of darkness won't accomplish the task. Heat and aggression are not valid substitutes for light and truth. Jesus equated good deeds with the shining of our light (Matthew 5:16). As His followers, we must draw others from the darkness by showing how much better it is to live in the light. Love, kindness, mercy, and unconditional friendship offer extremely high-wattage illumination. Like lighthouses, we will rescue more imperiled souls by shining a bright light than by sounding a loud horn. Talk is cheap if it isn't backed up by a life of good deeds.

SERVE OTHERS HUMBLY

"Serve" is another word to live by. Jesus taught His disciples that "whoever wants to become great among you must be your servant, and whoever wants to be first must be slave of all" (Mark 10:43, 44). The apostle Paul echoed Jesus' teaching when he exhorted us to "serve one another in love" (Galatians 5:13).

After the 9-11-01 terrorists attacks, America got a glimpse and taste of service. Firefighters and police worked long hours at Ground Zero in New York City to rescue survivors and recover bodies. Individuals and relief organizations served meals, doctors and nurses rendered assistance, and millions of citizens donated money to help victims' families. Also, in a great show of compassion, the United States Government dropped thousands of tons of food and supplies to Afghans displaced in the War against Terror. What Shakespeare called "the milk of human kindness" flowed in full measure across America.

Jesus' followers can set an example of service in a variety of ways. Service may be performed by baking a dozen cookies for an elderly neighbor. Sandwiches made and delivered to the homeless may show some needy hearts the love of Jesus. A hospital visit may touch a life. Clearing snow from a widow's sidewalk can be an act of service in Jesus' name. A poor family may welcome a sack of groceries or clothes for the kids. Serving an unemployed parent may consist of supplying a good lead for a job. Repairing a struggling single person's car is an act of service. So is babysitting a neighbor's children so Mom can go shopping without having little kids hanging on to her or worse still, hiding in clothes racks. Compassion and creativity can produce at least a thousand ways to minister to others in Jesus' name. It has been observed that if you want to improve your lot in life, build a service station on it.

MAKE DISCIPLES

Have you watched *the Antiques Roadshow* on television? It offers an intriguing glimpse into the human mind and values. Occasionally, an owner shows obvious dismay when an appraiser explains that an object is merely a counterfeit replica. Viewers can almost see dollar signs flash from $20,000, the owner's perceived value, to $10, the actual value. Sometimes, an owner learns that an object handed down through several generations is worth $30,000-$40,000. But the owner plans to keep it in the family. She will pass it on to her children.

Believers in every generation from the time of Jesus have inherited a treasure of incalculable worth. It is the privilege and responsibility of making disciples. Before ascending to heaven, Jesus told His disciples, "All authority in heaven and on earth has been given to me. Therefore go and make disciples of all nations, baptizing them in the name of the Father, and of the Son and of the Holy Spirit, and teaching them to obey everything I have commanded you. And surely I am with you always, to the very end of the age" (Matthew 28:18-20). These are powerful, imperative words to live by.

Some generations of Christians have done a better job of making disciples than have other generations. The Book of Acts reports that the first generation of Christians "preached the word wherever they went" (Acts 8:4). It did so in spite of intense persecution. The generations of disciples who spread the gospel during the Reformation and era of modern missions did a good job too. Martin Luther ignited Reformation fires by declaring that "the just shall live by faith," and John Knox exhibited the zeal of a true disciple-maker when he prayed, "Give me Scotland or I die." Later, William Carey, the humble shoemaker who became known as "the father of modern missions," left England and devoted his life to teaching and translating the Bible into numerous dialects in India.

The chapter has yet to close on our generation's performance as disciple-makers. Our nation and the world seem to be at a crossroads in history. Threats of bio-terrorism, nuclear weapons, wars, disease, and famine loom large. Traditional marriage and family life face enormous challenges, and kids are exposed to scandals and a number of media poisons, including Internet smut. We cannot legislate morality or force our lifeview on others, but we can show and tell what Jesus means to us. Friendly persuasion is a powerful discipling tool. If we use it wisely, history may record that our generation discipled America and other nations as well.

Interactive Discipleship

ANSWER THE FOLLOWING QUESTIONS:

1. What is your favorite Bible passage? Why?

2. Of all Jesus' sayings, which one has influenced your life the most? Why?

3. What do you think America would be like without the influence of the Bible?

4. Why do you suppose Jesus used simple language when He taught?

5. In 25 words or less tell what it means to follow Jesus.

6. Can a plumber, an attorney, and a homemaker follow Jesus as closely as a member of the clergy? Explain.

7. What has been your greatest reward for following Jesus?

8. What evidence of spiritual darkness do you see in contemporary life?

9. How can you shed your light around you?

10. What steps will you take this week to make disciples?

READ WHAT THE FOLLOWING PASSAGES SAY ABOUT WORDS TO LIVE BY:

Psalms 19: 7-11; 93; 111:7-10; 119:105-112, 129-136; Jeremiah 15:15, 16; Matthew 5:17-20; 7:24-29; Romans 10:11-15

MAKE DISCIPLES.

- Share this chapter with a friend.
- Huddle with a few followers of Jesus and discuss what you can do to oppose moral and spiritual darkness.
- Perform at least five acts of kindness this week.
- Agree with a friend to memorize the Beatitudes (Matthew 5:3-12). Set a goal of memorizing two beatitudes per week, and test each other at the end of each week.

MULL IT OVER.

Shakespeare wrote wisely about life and relationships. Who doesn't appreciate his words, "The quality of mercy is not strained. It droppeth as the gentle rain from heaven"? More recent communicators have given us powerful and memorable words. Four decades ago, President John F. Kennedy challenged, "Ask not what your country can do for you, but ask rather what you can do for your country." After the terrorist attacks of 9-11-02, President George W. Bush observed, "Americans are asking: What is expected of us? I ask you to live your lives, and hug your children. I know many citizens have fears tonight, and I ask you to be calm and resolute, even in the face of a continuing threat." But even the finest words written or spoken by human beings pale in comparison to Jesus' words. His words are true, infallible, and appropriate for all of us all the time. They are words to live by now and eternally.

PEACE THAT
GUARDS
THE HEART

Obtaining peace, whether international or personal, seems to be an illusive quest. Nearly every corner of the globe can be reached by phone or
e-mail, but remains beyond the reach of peace.
Reports of skirmishes, bombings, and outright
war grab our headlines and dominate our TV news
programs. In its search for peace of mind the public invests millions on books, courses, counseling
sessions, and prescriptions. Some attempts to find
peace of mind are pathetic but humorous. For example, a newspaper ad encouraged readers to sign
up for a peace-through-nature hike. For $85 par-
ticipants could join a hike along a fast-moving
mountain stream. At one point the hikers would
remove their shoes and socks and get in touch with
nature. Each person would find a stick and transfer
all his anxieties onto the stick. Then he would toss

it into the stream and watch it drift farther and farther away, until it disappeared from his sight. The participants would be encouraged to visualize all their cares drifting away and disappearing.

Oh, yes, a box lunch would be provided. So the $85 fee would not be an entire waste!

PEACE ON EARTH

Can peace settle over the world? Yes. Someday, Jesus, the Prince of Peace, will reign over the earth as King of kings and Lord of lords. The prophet Isaiah predicted that "the government will be on his shoulders . . . Of the increase of his government and peace there will be no end" (Isaiah 9:6, 7). Even the animal kingdom will enjoy tranquility when Jesus rules our planet. Dog and cat fights will be history. Even "the wolf will live with the lamb, the leopard will lie down with the goat, the calf and the lion and the yearling together . . . . The cow will feed with the bear, their young will lie down together, and the lion will eat straw like the ox" (11:6-8). "The infant will "play near the hole of the cobra, and the young child put his hand into the viper's nest" (verse 8). As for the nations, "they will beat their swords into plowshares and their spears into pruning hooks. Nation will not take up sword against nation, nor will they train for war anymore" (2:4).

Jesus will restore our planet to conditions similar to the peaceful and harmonious conditions that existed in the Garden of Eden.

JUDICIAL PEACE

The Bible promises two kinds of peace, both of which are essential to a purposeful, fulfilling life. They are peace with God and the peace of God. The moment a person believes in Jesus, he enters a peaceful relationship with God. God forgives that person's sins and accepts him into His forever family. He becomes what the Bible describes as "justified."

If you are familiar with text preparation, you know what "justified" means. You can choose to set your text justified. If you select justified, your text will be perfectly aligned on the page.

Here is an example of text that is unjustified on the left. It is called ragged left.

Bill is a house builder with a big problem. His walls, windows, and doors are always crooked. After Bill completes the framing stage of construction, his work fails the inspection. He has to hire another carpenter to redo it. All Bill's closest friends gently but firmly advise him to find a new job.

Here is the same text ragged right.

Bill is a house builder with a big problem. His walls, windows, and doors are always crooked. After Bill completes the framing stage of construction, his work fails the inspection. He has to hire another carpenter to redo it. All Bill's closest friends gently but firmly advise him to find a new job.

Here it is justified left and right.

Bill is a house builder with a big problem. His walls, windows, and doors are always crooked. After Bill completes the framing stage of construction, his work fails the inspection. He has to hire another carpenter to redo it. All Bill's closest friends gently but firmly advise him to find a new job.

Those who are justified with God are perfectly aligned with His righteousness. He sees no imperfections in them, because He has forgiven their sins and given them the complete righteousness of His Son Jesus. The apostle Paul affirmed these truths. He wrote, "Therefore, since we have been justified through faith, we have peace with God through our Lord Jesus Christ" (Romans 5:1), and he testified that "God made him [Jesus] who had no sin to be sin for us, so that in him we might become the righteousness of God" (2 Corinthians 5:21).

A missionary explained how the word "righteousness" is written in the Japanese language. The character for "lamb" is inscribed over the character for "us." The imagery is striking. Jesus' followers enjoy a righteous standing in God's sight and therefore peace with God because the Lamb of God is over us.

The prophet Isaiah, writing about 725 years before the birth of Jesus, linked peace with God and the sacrifice of Jesus, the Lamb of God. He foretold, "He was pierced for our transgressions, he was crushed for our iniquities; the punishment that brought us peace was upon him" (Isaiah 53:5).

PERSONAL PEACE

But Jesus not only made peace between God and us, He made it possible for us to experience divine peace every day. He promised, "Peace I leave with you; my peace I give you" (John 14:27). This use of the present tense "leave" and "give" affirms His peace is available now. Indeed, the Master's plan for you includes personal peace.

Jesus demonstrated His peace-producing power to His disciples in a special way one evening. He and His men were crossing the Sea of Galilee when a violent storm struck. It whipped the waves into a frenzy and lashed at the boat carrying Jesus and the disciples. Walls of water broke over the boat, nearly swamping it. But Jesus slept soundly in the stern—until the terrified disciples awoke Him. "Teacher, don't you care if we drown?" they asked.

Jesus stood up, rebuked the wind, and commanded the waves to settle down. "Quiet! Be still!" He ordered (Mark 4:39). Immediately, the storm ceased, and the sea became as smooth as glass.

Perhaps you have been caught in a terrifying storm and wished you had the power to command it to stop. But only Jesus has the authority and power to command storms to cease.

During a particularly distressing windstorm, two neighbors were tying down young trees in their backyards. "Hey," shouted one neighbor to the other. You're a pastor. Can't you do something to stop this terrible storm?"

"Sorry, Bob," the pastor shouted back, "I'm in Advertising not Production."

Sometimes storms crash upon us that no one—not

even a pastor—can subdue, but Jesus can do what no one else can. He can send sunshine to the soul in the thick of an angry storm. He can say with authority, "Quiet! Be still!"

The need for personal peace, the peace only Jesus can give, is profound. Dr. Richard Nakamura, acting director of the National Institute of Mental Health, reports that it is estimated that 5 to 10 percent of the U.S. population has major depression, and most people are not being helped. Worldwide, depression ranks fourth as a cause of disability.

Lydia Lewis, executive director of the National Depressive and Manic Depressive Association, states, "There are now three suicides to every two homicides in this country. I was shocked this year to see that suicide made it on the list of the ten most prevalent causes of death in the U.S., replacing AIDS."

Although some forms of depression may be linked to physiological causes, one cannot deny the fact that many individuals are depressed because they feel overwhelmed by the stresses of modern life and helpless to do anything about it. Those men and women need to know that Jesus' offer of peace can make a big difference in their lives.

Horatio Spafford, a Chicago businessman in the mid 1800s, had enjoyed great success until he lost almost everything in the great Chicago fire. After the fire, he decided to relocate his family. At 2 a.m., November 22, 1873, he boarded his wife and four daughters onto a French luxury liner, and agreed to rejoin them in France as soon as he could settle his business matters. A few days later, an English ship rammed the French ship and sent it to the ocean floor! Spafford's four daughters were among the 226 drowning victims.

Nine days later, the rescued survivors reached Cardiff, Wales. From Cardiff, Spafford's wife wired her husband. Her brief message read, "Saved alone."

The grieving Spafford booked passage on a ship to Europe to join his wife. On the voyage, the ship's Captain summoned Spafford to the bridge and pointed to the alleged spot where Spafford's daughters had drowned. Spafford retreated to his cabin, and wrote:

> *"When peace, like a river, attendeth my way,*
>
> *When sorrows, like sea billows roll,*
>
> *Whatever my lot, Thou hast taught me to say,*
>
> *'It is well, it is well with my soul.'"*

If you had known David T, you would have been impressed with his inner peace. It reflected the full measure of peace Jesus gives to those who love Him. For more than 50 years, David was confined to a wheelchair and unable to move more than his head and the index finger and thumb on his right hand. Doctors had predicted he would not live to see age 20. However, David proved them wrong. He lived far beyond 20 and never complained about his disability. Instead, he exuded a cheerfulness and positive attitude rarely matched by even the most physically fit members of society. He owned and operated a successful insurance agency, attended church regularly, served on the church board, and taught an adult Bible class. His mother was David's devoted and excellent caregiver until he died recently at the age of 60. Now in her 80s, she continues to exhibit the peace that only Jesus can give. Her pleasant personality and smile communicate a deep sense of peace to others. Speaking about her son's death, she recalled, "When David was a little boy, he said he was looking forward to going to heaven someday and being welcomed there by Jesus. 'Jesus will take my hand,' David said, 'and together we'll walk all around heaven.' Now, David is there and walking with Jesus."

David and his mother are just two of many unsung heroes of faith. Many others, who love and obey Jesus, face daily challenges, whether physical, emotional, occupational, or financial, with peace and optimism. They have learned to cast all their anxiety upon the Lord, knowing He cares for them (I Peter 5:7).

The apostle Peter, who encouraged us to cast all our anxiety on the Lord, practiced what he preached. The religious authorities who opposed first-century followers of Jesus, apprehended him more than once and beat him. Nevertheless, Peter responded each time with joy and peace. Nothing ruffled his sense of well-being. Even when he was imprisoned by Herod and marked for execution, Peter stayed calm. The threat of an executioner's sword severing his head from his body didn't keep Peter from enjoying a good night's sleep. He slept so soundly, as a matter of fact, that an angel dispatched to rescue him had to poke him in the ribs to wake him up (see Acts 12:6, 7).

The apostle Paul, too, enjoyed Jesus' peace in the midst of alarming circumstances. Although he was a prisoner of the Roman Empire and knew he might be martyred, he remained unperturbed. His inspired letter to the Philippians, written from prison, overflows with joy and the admonition to experience "the peace of God, which transcends all understanding" (Philippians 4:7).

About a month after terrorists struck the World Trade Center and the Pentagon and caused the downing of a passenger plane in Pennsylvania, President George Bush stepped to the pitcher's mound at Yankee Stadium and threw the first ball of the World Series. In the wake of vicious terrorist attacks and threats of more attacks, the President set a high mark for all Americans. He demonstrated personal tranquility and courage and sent a message to all Americans to go about their business and personal lives without fear.

Jesus' peace allowed His first-century disciples to go about the work of making disciples without fear. Although they faced a hostile world and the threats of persecution and even death, they forged ahead and sent a message to all of us who follow Jesus. Even when the way seems rough, we can carry on the work of making disciples with Jesus' peace in our hearts.

Interactive Discipleship

ANSWER THE FOLLOWING QUESTIONS:

1. What do you think the prospects are for world peace in your lifetime? Explain your reasoning.

2. How plausible is it for a person to experience lasting peace without believing on Jesus? Explain.

3. In what ways do people try to obtain peace?

4. If you could write a book on how to have peace, what would your opening words be?

5. What makes Jesus' peace different from peace of mind sought by such means as meditation and yoga?

6. How will our planet be different when Jesus rules the nations?

7. How have you experienced Jesus' peace in a recent trial?

8. How would you respond if a neighbor asked you how to have peace with God?

9. What does it mean to you to be justified with God?

10. How can you model personal peace this week?

READ WHAT THE FOLLOWING PASSAGES SAY ABOUT PEACE:

Psalms 4:1-8; 29:1-11; 119:161-168; Isaiah 26:1-3; 48:17-22; Luke 2:8-14; John 16:29-33; Acts 10:34-43; Colossians 3:12-17; James 3:13-18

MAKE DISCIPLES.

+ Share this chapter with a friend.

+ Pray for peace in your community and in the world.

+ Agree with a friend to memorize John 14:27 this week. At the end of the week discuss together situations in which you experienced Jesus' peace.

- ◆ Write a brief poem about personal peace and share it with someone who is going through a difficult time.
- ◆ Write a letter to an editor in which you comment on unrest in the world and identify Jesus as the giver of true and lasting personal peace.

MULL IT OVER.

"When Paul says 'the peace of God . . . shall keep your hearts,' he is using the figure of a citadel before which the Roman soldier stands sentry duty. Those living in the citadel have no fear of what is going on outside because they trust the sentry to keep them from danger and to warn them of the approach of an adversary. What the apostle is describing here is not so much delivering the mind after it has been obsessed with worry. He is promising that the mind will be kept from worry, because that which normally would cause concern is immediately transferred to the shoulder of One who is able to bear it for us."

—J. Dwight Pentecost, *The Joy of Living*
(Zondervan, Grand Rapids, 1973)

ATTITUDES THAT SHIELD THE MIND

"He needs an attitude adjustment."

You've heard this statement, haven't you? It may arise in a teachers' conference during a discussion about a certain fifth-grader who bullies classmates and sasses his teachers. It may be what a distraught parent says about a rebellious teenager. It may be how a manager describes a disgruntled employee to the Human Resources Director. It may even be what a dog owner reports to an animal trainer about her terrier terror. Whatever the situation, a bad attitude causes concern and needs to be adjusted before it erupts into a major crisis.

Christians are not exempt from the poison of a bad attitude. Sometimes a bad attitude leads to gossip, malice, negative criticism, and complaining. At other times it may break out in narrow-minded bigotry, egocentric behavior, resistance to change, or an unwillingness to cooperate. Resentment, bitterness, grudge bearing, and spite are further evidences of a bad attitude. Those who show any of these signs definitely need an attitude adjustment.

That's where Jesus' teachings enter the picture. He demonstrated a perfect attitude at all times—even in the worst circumstances. His attitude, as well as His actions, pleased His heavenly Father. No wonder the apostle Paul wrote, "Your attitude should be the same as that of Christ Jesus" (Philippians 2:5). Fortunately for us, Jesus revealed how we can have an attitude like His.

BE GRATEFUL

Gratitude is an attitude. It cannot be forced on anyone, nor does it spring naturally from affluence. It grows in the heart as we contemplate God's goodness and sense how much we owe to His grace. We can be grateful even if our money runs out, our health gives out, and our friends duck out. The apostle Paul had barely two shekels to rub together, he seemed to suffer poor health, and many of his friends deserted him, but he counseled us to, "give thanks in all circumstances" (I Thessalonians 5:18). Jesus lived a simple life. He was born in a stable and was cradled in a feeding trough. He owned no property, lived simply, walked almost everywhere, had only one item of clothing when He died, and was buried in a borrowed tomb. Yet, throughout His life, He demonstrated a grateful attitude. Before miraculously distributing five bread rolls and two tiny fish to 5,000 hungry followers, He gave thanks (John 6:11). After 70 disciples returned from a preaching mission, He gave thanks (Luke 10:17-21). He gave thanks for answered prayer at the raising of Lazarus (John 11:41). He offered thanks, too, when He shared the Passover meal with His disciples (Matthew 26:27).

Even when our circumstances seem bleak, we can maintain a grateful attitude by focusing our thoughts on God's favor. As we remember His past blessings to us and count our present ones, we realize how kind He is. Our troubles seem as small as a molehill when we lay them against the mountain of blessings God has piled into our lives. King David encountered numerous struggles and hardships in his life, yet he wrote, "Your love is ever before me" (Psalm 26:3). His attention was riveted not on his troubles but on the Lord's favor. So he was prepared to proclaim aloud the Lord's praise and tell of all His wonderful deeds (verse 7).

The author of the following poem understood that trials diminish in our eyes as we focus on God's blessings.

"When you have truly thanked your God

For every blessing sent,

But little time will then remain

For murmur or lament."

Media interviews with survivors of the September 11 attacks on the World Trade Center revealed a common theme—gratitude. Survivor after survivor expressed appreciation for his or her loved ones and a thankfulness to be alive and able to hug family members. The tragedy brought to light the uncertainty of life and the importance of making every day count. Survivors look at life differently. They have learned not to "sweat the small stuff," but to cherish what matters most.

We, too, can learn this lesson and offer thanks to our heavenly Father for what truly matters.

BE HUMBLE

Have acquaintances given you their resumes to pass on to your manager or Human Resources Department? Perhaps upon reading the resumes, you thought, *Wow, I didn't know she was so talented and knowledgeable. With such unrivaled qualifications, why doesn't she apply for an ambassadorship or the position of CEO at IBM?*

You may have watched a televised interview of a college football running back and heard him say, "I know I can score touchdowns if I'm handed the ball. I have great moves, run fast, don't fumble, and I'm hard to bring down. I hope today's game gives me lots of opportunities to showcase my skills. I know what I can do. Those who are watching today are going to see that I'm definitely NFL material."

Maybe you work with someone who brags constantly about his accomplishments. "You can thank me for the new color printer. I'm the one who talked the boss into spending the money for it," he boasts. "I'm top salesman again," he reports. "Maybe I should put a brass sign on my desk that reads, 'Definitely the best. I outsell the rest!'"

The three situations just cited may have something in common, but it definitely is not humility. A humble person may be talented—even gifted—and perform well, but he doesn't run a one-man admiration society. Humility is a virtue; egoism is a vice. The humble person has learned that the least important word in the English language is "I."

John the Baptist possessed a humble attitude, and Jesus said concerning him, "I tell you the truth: Among those born of women there has not risen anyone greater" (Matthew 11:11). The most important pronoun in John's language was not first person singular but third person singular. He confessed, "He [Jesus] must become greater; I must become less" (John 3:30). When John was baptizing his repentant countrymen, he announced that the arrival of the Messiah [Jesus] was imminent, He proclaimed: "I baptize you with water for repentance. But after me will come one who is more powerful than I, whose sandals I am not fit to carry" (Matthew 3:11).

Jesus, too, was humble. Although He had no sin and therefore no reason to repent, He humbly presented himself to John for baptism. Jesus knew His Father's will for the nation of Israel directed every Jew to be baptized. Because Jesus was a Jew, He complied with the Father's will (Matthew 3:15). He further demonstrated humility by assuming the role of a slave and washing His disciples' feet (John 13). Although the religious bureaucrats considered themselves too good to eat with tax collectors and sinners, Jesus ate with them (Matthew 8:10, 11). He made Himself available to the poor, the afflicted, the hungry, the hurting, and the alienated. He invited all the weary and burdened to "come to me . . . and I will give you rest" (Matthew 11:28). He explained: "I am gentle and humble in heart, and you will find rest for your souls" (verse 29).

Indeed, Jesus' entire life on earth was a saga of humility. Who can fathom how humbling it must have been for the Son of God to leave heaven and be born on earth as a helpless baby? In heaven He had been the object of angelic worship; on earth, the object of human scorn. In heaven He was honored as the possessor and sustainer of all things; on earth He was hated by the Pharisees and scribes. In heaven He enjoyed face-to-face fellowship with the Father; at Calvary the Father turned away from Him. In heaven He wore a crown; on earth, at Calvary, He wore a crown of thorns. In heaven He occupied a celestial throne; on earth, at Calvary, He occupied a criminal's cross. In heaven He lived as the eternal Sovereign; on earth He lived as a suffering servant. In heaven sinless heavenly beings worshiped Him; on earth sinful human beings crucified Him.

Theologians refer to the description of Jesus Christ found in Philippians 2:6-8 as the *kenosis*—the self-emptying of Christ. When He came to earth, He did not cease to be God, but He voluntarily laid aside the independent exercise of His divine prerogatives and lived in complete dependence on His Father. Read Philippians 2:6-8 carefully and ponder the exhortation that precedes this passage: "Your attitude should be the same as that of Jesus Christ" (verse 5).

"Who, being in very nature of God, did not consider equality with God something to be grasped, but made himself nothing [*eauton ekenosen*—emptied Himself], taking the very nature of a servant, being made in human likeness. And being found in appearance as a man, he humbled himself and became obedient to death—even death on a cross."

James McDougall, a Scotsman, had poured much time and energy into the sermon that would show in part that he was qualified for the ministry. He was confident that his words, voice, and gestures would make a very favorable impression on his audience. As he mounted the stairs leading to the church platform and pulpit, his confidence and pride were evident in his face and stride. However, disaster befell his sermon. His words came slowly and haltingly. At times he forgot what he had planned to say. His sermon notes fell to the floor.

After delivering his sermon, the young preacher descended the stairs painstakingly. His head hung low. "What went wrong?" he asked Robin Malair, the church's elderly sexton.

"Well, laddie," Robin offered, "if ye gone up as ye came doon, ye'd a come doon as ye went up."

"I am gentle and humble of heart," Jesus said. How can we, His followers, be something different?

BE POSITIVE

Our Master wants us to maintain a positive attitude as well as a grateful and humble attitude. Often, He said, "Fear not." A negative attitude reflects fear and admits defeat. But a positive attitude reflects faith and claims victory. Believers with a negative attitude wring their hands and cry out, "Poor me!" But believers with a positive attitude fold their hands in prayer and cry out, "Praise God!" Negative-minded people look at a rose bush and see the thorns, whereas positive-minded people look at a rose bush and see the roses.

Research has shown that a smiley face drawn on a restaurant check increases a waitress's tips by 18 percent and a waiter's tips by 3 percent. We can only guess the effect of a frowning face on a check.

Of course, someone with a negative attitude is likely to ask what he has to smile about. "The weather is lousy," he moans, "and the world is falling apart." But the positive person sings, "Those April showers, they bring May flowers," and exclaims, "Let's do something for Jesus that will make our world better."

A negative believer shakes his head from side to side, stoops his shoulders, pouts, and groans, "Aunt Mildred is so set her ways it's useless to talk to her about Jesus. She would never become one of His followers. You might as well try to find a clean table in a rundown fast food restaurant as try to find a soft spot in her heart." A positive believer, on the other hand, says, "Aunt Mildred may be set in her ways and a bit hardhearted, but I'm trusting Jesus to give me the right words to say to her. No one lies beyond the reach of God's love. I think Aunt Mildred can become a joyful follower of Jesus."

Jesus encouraged positive thinking. Here is a brief list of some of His teachings that encourage a positive attitude:

- "Do not worry . . . " (Matthew 6:25, 31, 34).
- "According to your faith will it be done to you" (Matthew 9:29).
- "Even the very hairs of your head are all numbered [by the heavenly Father]. So don't be afraid" (Matthew 10:30, 31).

- "All things are possible with God" (Mark 10:27).

- "Everyone who has left houses or brothers or sisters or father or mother or children or fields for my sake will receive a hundred times as much and will inherit eternal life" (Matthew 19:29).

- "Whoever believes in me, as the Scripture has said, streams of living water will flow from within him" (John 7:38).

- "Do not let your hearts be troubled" (John 14:1).

- "I will ask the Father, and he will give you another Counselor to be with you forever—the Spirit of truth" (John 14:16).

- "Peace I leave with you" (John 14:27).

- In this world you will have trouble. But take heart! I have overcome the world" (John 16:33).

- "Ask and your joy will be complete" (John 16:24).

- "All authority in heaven and on earth has been given to me. Therefore go and make disciples of all nations . . . . And surely I am with you always, to the very end of the age" (Matthew 28:18-20).

Likely, many individual believers and churches would achieve greater success in making disciples if they focused on the positive statements and promises Jesus gave. Bemoaning our lack of resources compared with those of others can waste much time and effort. All congregational dirges sound alike. They chant, "We have a poor location," or "Our people aren't rich," or "Our facilities aren't attractive," or "We don't have enough musical talent," or

"We can't possibly offer the programs First Church offers." What might happen, though, if believers in a growth-challenged congregation developed a positive attitude about the authority Jesus placed behind His command to go and make disciples? What if they stopped being obstinate and started being obedient? What if they scuttled negative thinking and assured one another that Jesus' promises guarantee victory in spite of the obstacles?

When Winston Churchill was Prime Minister of England during World War II, he delivered stirring speeches to the British people encouraging them not to quit but to fight on against the Germans. Even as he walked among the bombed ruins of London, he predicted victory and flashed the V for victory sign. His winning attitude lifted Britain's spirits and led the nation to victory.

A small-town barber and father of six children enjoyed a fine business, one that allowed him to support his family comfortably. He enjoyed a sizable customer base and charged $10 a haircut. Then a hair salon opened across from his. Because it was part of a big chain of hair salons, it was able to advertise, "Any haircut, $8."

Gradually, the barber's business declined, leaving him with only a few loyal customers, unpaid household bills, and a case of self-pity. But just when he was on the verge of throwing in his barber's towel and closing his establishment, a friend suggested he make a big sign and hang it over his shop. The friend even suggested appropriate wording. The barber took his friend's advice, and soon his former customers were filing back into his place of business.

What did the sign read? "We fix $8 haircuts."

Positive-minded followers of Jesus are proactive. Problems are simply challenges, and challenges are opportunities to find solution.

BE MINDFUL OF OTHERS

The Master's plan for you and every disciple includes having an attitude of being mindful of others. Self-centered thinking is foreign to righteousness and never enjoys God's blessing. Jesus taught us to love and serve others. He said, "By this all men will know that you are my disciples, if you love one another" (John 13:35). He also endorsed the command to love our neighbor but extended it to include loving our enemies (Matthew 5:43, 44). That's a tall order, but it is not out of reach. God plants His love in our hearts and enables us to place others' needs ahead of our own (Romans 5:5; 12:10, 20; Galatians 6:10; Philippians 2:3, 4). "Whoever wants to become great among you," Jesus told His disciples, "must be your servant" (Mark 10:43).

A Christian doctor, who devoted his professional life to helping the poor, lived and practiced above a delicatessen. He never asked for payment from any patient who was too poor to afford his medical attention, and his fee to others was far below that of any other doctor in town. A sign outside the delicatessen announced *Dr. Johnson is upstairs.*

When the good doctor died, he left no money or property. He had no relatives, and he left no money for his burial, but his patients contributed enough money from their meager funds to bury him. They could not afford a tombstone, however. So it seemed Dr. Johnson's grave would stay unmarked, until someone offered a creative idea.

A couple of the patients removed the doctor's sign from in front of the delicatessen and fastened it to a post over his grave. The epitaph was clear to all: *Dr. Johnson is upstairs.*

Following Jesus involves a life of service now and in heaven as well. As someone remarked, "The pay may not be so great, but the benefits and retirement are out of this world.

Harry Bullis, former CEO of General Mills, advised his sales force to start every day with the thought, *I want to help as many people as possible today,* instead of, *I want to make as many sales as possible today.* Bullis explained that his sales representatives would receive a better reception and make more sales.

The goal of serving others and the goal of making disciples intertwine. As we perform deeds of love and kindness in obedience to Jesus' command to let our light shine, we gain an entry to hearts and minds. For many the adventure of following Jesus begins when they see His love demonstrated in the lives of those who believe in Him.

Interactive Discipleship

ANSWER THE FOLLOWING QUESTIONS:

1. What is the strongest aspect of your attitude? the weakest? What steps will you take to improve your attitude?

2. Name five things you are most grateful for.

3. What happens to your attitude when you thank God for specific blessings?

4. How do you feel when someone thanks you for a kindness you performed?

5. Should you try to get something from God by praising Him? Why or why not?

6. Why do you agree or disagree that you have to brag on yourself to get ahead in life?

7. What do you see as differences between meekness and weakness?

8. What do you see as some damaging effects of being negative?

9. How can you maintain a positive attitude in an evil world?

10. Who needs your prayers right now? How can praying for that person or those individuals be an act of service?

READ WHAT THE FOLLOWING PASSAGES SAY ABOUT THE POWER OF THE THOUGHT LIFE FOR EITHER GOOD OR EVIL:

Genesis 6 1-7; Psalm 94:1-11; 139:17-24; Proverbs 12:1-20; Isaiah 59:1-8; Mark 7:9-20; 2 Corinthians 10:1-5; Philippians 2:1-11; Hebrews 4:1-13; James 2:1-4

MAKE DISCIPLES.

- Share this chapter with a friend.

- Spread a good attitude around your home, congregation, place of employment, and neighborhood.

- Ask a trusted friend to share attitude perceptions with you, then pray together for improvements in needy areas.

- Volunteer to take an elderly person shopping or to lunch or to church or to an appointment. Be at that person's service.

MULL IT OVER.

If God were to give you a report card that included His evaluation of your attitude, would you score S for Satisfactory, U for Unsatisfactory, or NI (Needs to Improve)? For each category below indicate the grade you think you would receive:

Cooperative, works well with others   _____

Has a positive attitude, is cheerful   _____

Cares about others, is unselfish   _____

Eager to learn   _____

Shows appreciation   _____

CHARACTER
THAT BLESSES
OTHERS

The Texas Seven had broken out of prison in
Texas, killed a police officer, and fled the state,
prompting a massive manhunt that ended quietly
in the Colorado Springs, Colorado, area. The fugitives had dyed their hair and managed to elude authorities by changing their modus operandi. After
paying cash for a mobile home, they presented roses the following day to the woman who had sold
it to them. They checked in at a mobile home park
in Woodland Park and appeared to be model resi-
dents. The park manager described them as polite
and friendly. Some members of the infamous sev-
en even attended a local Bible study. But when
"America's Most Wanted" TV program featured
them, the park manager recognized them and no-
tified the authorities. Soon six of the seven were
in custody. The seventh committed suicide rather

than surrender to police. The fugitives' character façade failed to alter the fact that they were desperadoes at heart, and ultimately their true character surfaced.

Sometimes, critics of Christianity hurl the term hypocrites at those who claim to follow Jesus. Perhaps the term fits some but not all. Genuine followers of Jesus are men and women of godly character, and their character is a source of blessing to others. If they do wrong, it is out of character. If they do right, it is in character. When they sin, they feel convicted, experience regret, quickly confess their sin, and seek God's help to follow Jesus more closely. Over the course of their lives as Jesus' disciples, their character becomes more like that of the Lord Jesus because the Holy Spirit shapes them into His image.

Matthew 5 includes Jesus' description of people with good character as "poor in spirit," "those who mourn," "meek," "those who hunger and thirst for righteousness," "merciful," "pure in heart," and "peacemakers." In spite of the fact that such people are often persecuted and maligned (verses 10, 11), they are "blessed" [spiritually prosperous, happy], and they will be richly rewarded by their heavenly Father.

Commenting on the word "blessed" in Matthew 5, Greek scholar Marvin R. Vincent indicates that having "passed into the higher region of Christian thought . . . it becomes the express symbol of a happiness identified with pure character" (*Word Studies in the New Testament*, Wm. B. Eerdmans Publishing Co., Grand Rapids, 1957, Vol. I, p. 35.)

POOR IN SPIRIT BUT SPIRITUALLY RICH

What does it mean to be "poor in spirit"? Is being poor in spirit a characteristic worth cultivating? After all, who wants to be poor?

Being poor in spirit is to acknowledge our total deficiency and inability to contribute anything to our salvation. We are poor in spirit when we see ourselves as destitute of the righteousness God requires for admission into heaven. Because we are poor in spirit, we trust in Jesus for salvation. We believe He paid the full penalty of our sin when He died on the cross, and we receive the righteousness He imparts to all who believe in Him (see Romans 3:22-26 and 4:5).

You may recall that when Jesus was hanging on the cross, He cried out, "It is finished" (John 19:30). These three words translate one Greek word, *tetelestai*, meaning, "It stands finished." In the ancient Greek world this word was often written on bills that were paid in full. A painter might use this word after applying a final dab of paint. Looking at his painting and feeling satisfied that nothing needed to be added to it, he would exclaim, "*Tetelestai.*" Similarly, nothing needs to be added to what Jesus did on the cross to obtain our salvation. Those who are poor in spirit recognize their spiritual bankruptcy and claim what Jesus did on the cross as their "paid-in-full" redemption.

If someone paid your mortgage in full and the mortgage company issued you written proof that the debt had been paid, would you continue to write a monthly check to the mortgage company? Of course not! You would thank your benefactor and celebrate your good fortune.

Similarly, those who are poor in spirit are happy that Jesus paid the debt of their sin, and they celebrate the transaction by serving Him joyfully all the days of their lives.

The apostle Peter captured the liberating truth of full redemption and appealed to his readers to live holy out of regard for what Jesus did for them. He wrote: "Be holy . . . live . . . in reverent fear. For you know that it was not with perishable things such as silver or gold you were redeemed from the empty way of life handed down to you from your forefathers, but with the precious blood of Christ, a lamb without blemish or defect" (I PeterI:16-19).

Being poor in spirit introduces us to the greatest exchange program of all time. We exchange spiritual poverty for spiritual riches, alienation from God for acceptance with God, condemnation for acquittal, sins for righteousness, helplessness for hope, and enmity with God for intimacy with God. No wonder Jesus said, "Blessed [spiritually prosperous, happy] are the poor in spirit."

Being poor in spirit, we enjoy the riches of God's blessings and can live as His instruments of blessing to others.

GOOD MOURNING!

"Blessed are those who mourn," Jesus said, "for they shall be comforted" (Matthew 5:4). What was Jesus talking about? Mourning ranks high, perhaps highest, as a distressful human emotion. How can anyone who mourns be happy (blessed)?

Jesus was referring to mourning over sin. Those who feel distressed by their sin can be happy in the midst of sadness, because they will be comforted when they seek forgiveness. Several centuries before Jesus came to earth, God promised His wayward people that the Messiah would arrive and bring comfort to the repentant. He urged in Isaiah 55:7, "Let the wicked forsake his way and the evil man his thoughts. Let him turn to the LORD, and he will have mercy on him, and to our God, for he will freely pardon." Isaiah 61:1-3 quotes Messiah in advance of His coming:

> "The Spirit of the Sovereign LORD is on me, because the LORD has anointed me to preach good news to the poor. He has sent me to bind up the brokenhearted, to proclaim freedom for the captives and release from darkness for the prisoners, to proclaim the year of the LORD'S favor and the day of vengeance of our God, to comfort all who mourn, and provide for those who grieve in Zion—to bestow on them a crown of beauty instead of ashes. The oil of gladness instead of mourning, and a garment of praise instead of a spirit of despair. They will be called oaks of righteousness, a planting of the LORD for the display of his splendor."

Jesus clearly identified Himself as the Messiah, whose coming to earth guaranteed the fulfillment of the prophecy given in Isaiah 61:1-3. About a year into His public ministry Jesus entered the synagogue at Nazareth, read aloud from Isaiah 61, and announced, "Today this scripture is fulfilled in your hearing" (Luke 4:21).

Although a few Jewish men and women repented of their sins and believed on Jesus as the Messiah during His life on the earth, the nation of Israel will not experience widespread mourning over sin and faith in Jesus until He comes to earthy again. Zechariah 12:10 describes the dramatic event: "And I will pour out on the house of David and the inhabitants of Jerusalem a spirit of grace and supplication. They will look on me, the one they have pierced, and they will mourn for him as one mourns for an only child, and grieve bitterly for him as one grieves for a first-born son."

Followers of Jesus have turned away from the path of sinning and are walking now in the path of righteousness, but they are not sinless. Occasionally, even the most devout disciples stumble and do what they know they shouldn't do or fail to do what they know they should do. Even the apostle Paul stumbled at times. He wrote, "For what I want to do I do not do, but what I hate I do" (Romans 7:15). Truly, followers of Jesus are not as good as they ought to be or as good as they are going to be, but they are not as bad as they used to be. However, when a follower of Jesus sins, he ought to mourn the fact, confess the sin, and embrace God's forgiveness. The apostle John highlighted the comfort that awaits repentant confessors. "If we confess our sins, he is faithful and just and will forgive our sins and purify us from all unrighteousness" (1 John 1:9).

The apostle James, too, wrote about mourning over sin and the subsequent comfort the mourner finds. He counseled:

"Come near to God and he will come near to you. Wash your hands, you sinners, and purify your hearts, you double-minded. Grieve, mourn and wail. Change your laughter to mourning and your joy to gloom. Humble yourselves before the Lord, and he will lift you up" (James 4:8-10).

Occasionally, a follower of Jesus loses his spiritual focus. Instead of keeping his eyes on Jesus, he gazes longingly at the momentary pleasures of sin. If he refuses to confess his sin and regain his spiritual focus, he experiences remedial discipline. The heavenly Father disciplines him so he will understand the folly of his way, confess his sin, and seek restoration. Hebrews 12:10,11 teaches, "Our fathers disciplined us for a little while as they thought best; but God disciplines us for our good, that we may share in his holiness. No discipline seems pleasant at the time, but painful. Later on, however, it produces a harvest of righteousness and peace for those who have been trained by it."

The believer who has mourned over sin and experienced the joy of forgiveness is well-positioned to bless others by assuring them that the best life has to offer is found right behind Jesus' footsteps.

It's Okay to Be Meek

Popular advice for our fast-paced times is, "Be tough, be assertive, put yourself first, look out for Numero Uno." Jesus' advice for all times is quite different. He said, "Blessed are the meek, for they will inherit the earth" (Matthew 5:5). But what does it mean to be meek? Does a meek person resemble a doormat? Is he a milksop? chopped liver? a wimp? Absolutely not! Jesus described Himself as meek ["gentle," NIV] (Matthew 11:28), but

He withstood a satanic onslaught of temptations after fasting 40 days and 40 nights. He also chased a horde of moneychangers from the temple. To be meek means to be in humble compliance with God's will. It is the opposite of self-will and spiritual rebellion.

Before cars, trucks, and tractors transformed transportation and increased the mobility and speed of modern life, horses did far more than strut their stuff in parades and compete in races. They pulled carriages. They dragged plows across fields. They carried riders. Mail, milk, bread, and a variety of goods arrived at people's homes by way of horse-drawn wagons. But those horses had to be "broken" before they were useful to their owners. A horse is not born with a passionate desire to drag a plow or carry a human on its back or pull a wagon. You just don't throw a bridle or harness or saddle on an untamed horse and expect to enjoy a carefree day. An untamed horse will kick, stomp, buck, throw its head back, flare its eyes, and even bite at the first sign of a bridle, harness, or saddle. But once a horse has been "broken," it abandons the fight and complies with its master's commands.

A man who enjoys memories of his father delivering bread house to house by horse and wagon relates that his father would leave the wagon, deliver bread to several houses, and whistle for the horse to bring the wagon to him. He remarked that a truck could never be so obliging.

Meekness stamps the character of every follower of Jesus who has submitted his will to the control of the Master. It is not natural to our nature, but is a characteristic produced by the ministry of the Holy Spirit (Galatians 5:22, 23).

Meek men and women receive the Lord's promise that they will inherit the earth (Matthew 5:5). Evil dictators often try to grab countries and dominate lives, but their efforts are doomed. Only Jesus has the right to claim our planet as His own, and someday He will oust all illegal claimants and take possession for Himself and His followers.

The promise that we shall receive such an inheritance frees us from a materialistic attitude. Why should we harbor greed or hold tightly to things that are merely temporal? Someday, we will inherit the earth. Until then we can throw ourselves into the eternally valuable task of obeying Jesus' command to make disciples.

IS ANYBODY HUNGRY OR THIRSTY?

It seems that most people get hungry or thirsty after working or playing hard. Granted, a few loners never seem to get hungry or thirsty. They sometimes work through the lunch hour. When asked why they didn't break for lunch, they reply, "I forgot all about lunch." Most of us would forget our own name quicker than we would forget lunch.

A good, strong spiritual appetite should mark every follower of Jesus. "Blessed are those who hunger and thirst for righteousness," Jesus said, "for they will be filled" (Matthew 5:6). Hungry and thirsty people have one thing on their minds: the goal of finding food and drink. Stranded and parched in a desert, wayfarers will crawl to an oasis. Deprived in a war-torn land, refugees will scuffle with others to reach food dropped from planes or tossed from the back of a truck. Homeless on a city street, men and women will resort to begging for the money to buy a sandwich and a cup of coffee. The need to be filled drives hungry people.

Does the need to be filled with righteousness drive us? Our newspapers relate stories of those who hungered for power, fame, wealth, popularity, self-fulfillment, and sex, only to discover emptiness and misery. Indeed, human history recounts personal tragedies that lurked at the end of a search for whatever the seekers believed would satisfy their hunger.

The Bible shows what happens to those who hunger for something God has placed off limits. The trail of misery extends from Adam in the garden to Satan and his followers at the end of time. Lot is just one example of a man who thought something other than righteousness would satisfy him. He severed ties with Abraham when he hungered for the good life he thought the fertile plains near the city of Sodom would bring. Eventually, he moved into Sodom and settled down there in spite of the wretched behavior of its citizens. But only trouble and loss met Lot in Sodom. First, he was taken hostage by a marauding coalition of enemy forces. Then, after being rescued by Abram, Lot, his wife, and two daughters were yanked out of Sodom by angels just before God consumed it with burning sulfur. Every material thing Lot had prized so highly went up in smoke. But Lot lost even more than material goods and property. He lost his wife. She disobeyed the instruction, "Don't look back." When she looked back, she was covered with burning, erupting salt deposits and became "a pillar of salt." Lot also lost all self-respect and personal sanctity when he got drunk and slept with his daughters. By contrast, Abram chose to pursue righteousness. He honored God, and committed his future to Him. God satisfied Abraham with righteousness and called him His friend (2 Chronicles 20:7; James 2:23).

If we look around us, we will see how hungry people are. If we hunger and thirst after righteousness, we will know the blessedness of being "filled." In turn we can introduce others to our Lord. The satisfaction He brings to our lives is something worth sharing!

MERCY, MERCY!

"Blessed are the merciful," Jesus announced (Matthew 5:7). This endorsement of showing mercy flew in the face of Roman thinking. The Romans equated mercy with weakness. They followed harsh rules and handed down stiff sentences to transgressors. But Jesus taught merciful compassion by word and example. If we choose to obey and emulate Him, we must be merciful.

Although many believers show merciful compassion by ministering to the needy, others choose to close their eyes and hearts to them. They spin a cocoon around them and withdraw into it. Their world includes only themselves, their families, and their church clique. They avoid the neighbor who is hurting emotionally or physically or financially. They cross to the other side of the street rather than face a homeless man or woman. They turn a deaf ear to starving refugees' pleas for help. They deride even legitimate welfare recipients. They are not even moved by Jesus' depiction of the lost as sheep scattered and not having a shepherd. They shun any member of the congregation who falls into sin, and they demand he be excommunicated. They prefer to shoot their own wounded rather than heed the instructions of Galatians 6:1: "Brothers, if someone is caught in a sin, you who are spiritual should restore him gently. But watch yourself, or you also may be tempted."

Evangelist Dwight L. Moody ministered compassionately to men and women of every rank and station. His attitude toward every Skid Row person he met was, "There, but by the grace of God, go I." He also said he could learn something from everyone who crossed his path. Instead of looking down on the less fortunate, Moody reached down and helped them.

A hospitalized or institutionalized person may open her heart's door to Jesus when a compassionate follower of Jesus visits her. A gift of flowers, a greeting card, or an offer to run an errand may be the door opener the Holy Spirit uses. A homeless person may become a follower of Jesus when he receives a box lunch and kind words. A coworker, soured on Christianity, may change his attitude when a believing coworker stays late to help him meet a deadline. A grieving widow, touched by a visit from a compassionate Christian neighbor, may turn in faith to Jesus and cast her burden on Him. Who can tell how many men and women in a sometimes-cold world will warm up to Jesus when His followers demonstrate His love in compassionate acts?

According to Jesus, the merciful will not only be happy but will also be the recipients of reciprocal treatment. "They will be shown mercy," Jesus promised. Our heavenly Father rewards merciful deeds by showering us with merciful favors. His compassion is boundless and His kindness is inexhaustible. He invites us to make our needs known to Him, and he promises to grant mercy and grace to "help us in our time of need" (Hebrews 4:16).

100% PURE

There's something appealing about a product advertised as 100% pure. You just can't beat the taste of 100% pure Vermont maple syrup poured generously over hot pancakes coated with 100% pure butter. Forget the 100% pure calories; the eating pleasure is 100% pure delight.

A 100% pure life is delightful too. Jesus said, "Blessed are the pure in heart, for they will see God (Matthew 5:8)." These words spoken by the Master rebuked the hypocrisy of the Pharisees who only pretended to be pure. They wore their religion on their sleeves and paraded their piety in public. They loved to perform religious deeds designed to draw praise from their fellow Jews, but they failed to pass the inspection of God, who sees the heart. King David wrote about the purity that God looks for in the lives of those who worship Him. "Surely you desire truth in the inner parts," he confessed (Psalm 51:6), and requested, "Create in me a pure heart, O God" (verse 10).

As David indicated, a pure heart is a divine creation. When a person believes on Jesus, he receives not only forgiveness and a righteous standing in God's sight but also a desire to be like Jesus (Romans 5:17-21; 2 Corinthians 5:17). From that moment, the Holy Spirit begins to develop godly characteristics in him. As the believer obeys Jesus, his new Master, his character increasingly resembles Jesus' character (see 2 Corinthians 3:17, 18; Galatians 5:22, 23; and 2 Peter 1:3-8).

However, no follower of Jesus will be 100% pure in his thoughts, desires, ambitions, motives, words, and deeds until he enters heaven, but every believer ought to be increasingly pure with every passing day. "Keep yourself pure," Paul instructed Timothy. And the apostle John assured us that every believer who anticipates seeing Jesus someday "purifies himself, just as he [Jesus] is pure" (I John 3:3).

Matthew 5:8 promises that the pure in heart will see God. Although the pure will see God in eternity, it is also true that they will see Him in this life. They will enjoy a perceptive understanding of Him because they will be close to Him. They will see His hand in the affairs of life. They will see His presence in their trials as well as in their triumphs. They will see His glory in the mountains, forests, wheat fields, streams, rivers, lakes, and ocean. They will see His wisdom in the orderly laws of nature. They will see His goodness in the air they breathe and in every provision He gives. They will see His manifold, infinite knowledge and power in the complexity of the human body and in the vast array of birds, fish, and animals. Arthur W. Pink suggests: "The pure in heart possess spiritual discernment and with their eyes of their understanding they obtain clear views of the Divine character and perceive the excellency of His attributes" (*An Exposition of the Sermon on the Mount*, Baker Book House, Grand Rapids, 1979, p. 34).

Having such a clear view of God equips the pure in heart for the responsibility of communicating God's character to their loved ones and casual acquaintances too. Being blessed, they can bless others.

A PIECE OF HEAVENLY PEACE

Jesus said, "Blessed are the peacemakers, for they will be called the sons of God" (Matthew 5:9). Unless we live with our heads in the sand and withdraw them only in the dead of night, we know the world can't grasp peace any better than greasy hands can grasp a glob of gelatin. Hostility and violence erupt in such places as the Middle East and Northern Ireland almost as soon as delegates hug and walk away from the negotiating table. Fighting, terrorism, and heated words stir tempers and fan hatred in countries small and large. But unrest and violence mar personal relationships too. Far too often, domestic disputes end in assault— even murder. A dismissed employee returns to his former jobsite, and armed with a weapon he guns down innocent coworkers. Even schools and sports venues aren't exempt from violence. We have all heard about high school shootings and/or bomb threats. We also learned of a hockey dad who was sentenced to prison for 6 to 10 years for beating another dad to death at a hockey game. And sad to say, nasty feelings and ugly quarrels break out occasionally even in churches.

So Jesus' followers face an enormous task as peacemakers. The apostle Paul urged us to live in harmony with one another," "If it is possible, as far as it depends on you, live at peace with everyone," and "Make every effort to keep the unity of the Spirit through the bond of peace" (Romans 12:16, 18; Ephesians 4:3). Christians who claim to believe in burying the hatchet but know exactly where they want to bury it ought to put aside their hostile feelings and pick up an olive branch.

Peacemaking opportunities abound. A faithful Christian couple can prayerfully and carefully help a quarreling couple resolve their differences and renew their marriage vows. A believing employee can help at-odds coworkers understand and respect their opposing viewpoints. A teenager devoted to Christ can befriend a loner at school and introduce him to a circle of friends. A believing parent can offer biblical counsel to the parent of a rebellious son or daughter. Every believer can make disciples, thereby bringing those who are alienated from God into a peaceful and friendly relationship with Him.

A reputation for peacemaking is priceless and powerful. Jesus said peacemakers "will be called sons of God" (Matthew 5:9). They do not have to call themselves sons of God; their ministry of resolving conflict will convince others that they are God's sons.

How persuasive is your character?

Do you savor the taste of corn on the cob, perhaps Golden Bantam corn on the cob smothered with butter and sprinkled with salt? Remarkably, all the Golden Bantam corn in American originated from a single stalk of corn on a Vermont hillside. Its discoverer preserved the seed and planted it year after year. Now the corn is readily available to be enjoyed by all who include it in their diet. Similarly, every follower of Jesus "planted" in a family, in a congregation, in a place of employment, in a neighborhood, and in a community, can reproduce spiritually by making disciples. Blessings can spread from a single obedient, productive life until an entire nation tastes and sees that the Lord is good.

Interactive Discipleship

ANSWER THE FOLLOWING QUESTIONS:

1. What evidences of genuine Christian character do you find most persuasive?

2. How does being poor in spirit relate to salvation?

3. Why shouldn't a person trust in his own righteousness to gain God's favor?

4. In your own words tell what you believe good mourning is.

5. Do you think today's disciples are becoming more concerned about sin in society? Sin in their own lives? Explain.

6. What kinds of discipline does God use to restore His disobedient children?

7. What do you see people hungering for?

8. How does Jesus satisfy your hunger for righteousness?

9. What aspects of God's character do you see most clearly?

10. How will you show mercy this week?

11. How will you act as a peacemaker this week?

12. Do you think it is futile to pray for world peace? Why or why not?

READ WHAT THE FOLLOWING PASSAGES SAY ABOUT CHARACTER:

Job 1:1-9; Psalms 34:11-22; 37:23-40; Proverbs 16:19-33; 31:10-31; Romans 12:9-21; Colossians 3:5-17; I Peter 5:1-10

MAKE DISCIPLES.

- Share this chapter with a friend.
- Invite a Christian friend to join you in compiling a list of Christlike characteristics and compare notes after two weeks to review opportunities you had to develop and display those characteristics.
- Show compassion this week by volunteering resources and time to help meet the needs of a poor family. Your church may be able to supply a family's name and address.
- Tell at least one person this week how to have peace with God.

MULL IT OVER.

When you get what you want in your struggle for self
And the world makes you king for a day,
Just go to the mirror and look at yourself
And see what that man has to say.

For it isn't your father or mother or wife
Whose judgment upon you must pass.
The fellow whose verdict counts most in your life
Is the one staring back from the glass.

You may be like Jack Horner and chisel a plum
And think you're a wonderful guy.
But the man in the glass says you're only a bum
If you can't look him straight in the eye.

He's the fellow to please—never mind all the rest,
For he's with you clear to the end.
And you've passed your most dangerous, difficult test
If the man in the glass is your friend.

You may fool the whole world down the pathway of years
And get pats on the back as you pass.
But your final reward will be heartache and tears
If you've cheated the man in the glass.

—AUTHOR UNKNOWN

WORK THAT HOLDS SIGNIFICANCE

The Seven Dwarfs set an example for all of us by singing and whistling as they went to work. "Hi ho! Hi ho! It's off to work we go!" Although they worked all day and got no pay, they were happy. Well, maybe Grumpy wasn't happy, but six out of seven isn't bad.

What's your attitude toward work? Maybe you sing, "I owe! I owe! It's off to work I go!" There is reason to be extremely happy, though, if you perceive your day job as part of the most significant work on the face of the planet. That hugely significant work is disciple making, and the risen Son of God is in charge of the project.

Jesus had poured much of His energy into training His disciples for the work of making disciples. He gave them three and a half years of personal training in which He taught them by precept and example how to communicate God's love and forgiveness. Graduation day came 40 days after His resurrection. On the Mount of Olives, He assured the disciples that He possessed "all authority in heaven and on earth" (Matthew 28:18), and commissioned them to go out into the world and "make disciples of all nations" (verse 19). First, however, they were to wait in Jerusalem for the arrival of the Holy Spirit, who would empower them for the task.

When the Holy Spirit came on the Day of Pentecost, He equipped the disciples (apostles) for the work Jesus had assigned. Three thousand men and women at Jerusalem welcomed the apostle Peter's presentation of Jesus as the Messiah and "signed on" to follow Jesus. From Jerusalem, the growing number of disciples spread the message of Jesus throughout Judea, Samaria, and the Roman Empire. The Book of Acts, which records the history of that early disciple-making effort, concludes by relating that the apostle Paul was in Rome and actively engaged in preaching the kingdom of God and teaching about the Lord Jesus Christ in spite of the fact that he was under house arrest (Acts 28:30, 31). Clearly, the zeal of making disciples burned intensely in the hearts of first-century believers.

REKINDLE THE FIRE!

Although disciple making continued to be the church's top priority throughout the first century, it lost momentum in the third and fourth centuries and from the fifth to fifteenth centuries was almost forgotten. Theological wrangling and ecclesiastical bureaucracy consumed much of the church's attention and energy until the Reformation in the sixteenth and seventeenth centuries restored the focus to the work of making disciples. Before the Reformation, for example, a group known as scholastics preferred to debate how many angels could dance on the head of pin rather than summon believers to step out in faith to disciple their communities. The era of modern missions and revival movements followed the Reformation and brought hope that disciple making would flourish throughout the church's lifetime, but today complacency has replaced the fervor of discipleship in far too many congregations. Yet, a growing number of believers are asking to be challenged and equipped to disciple themselves and others. Tired of ever learning and never doing, they want to rekindle the fire of disciple making that burned in the first-century church.

What can you do to help build a roaring fire?

♦ *Realize that disciple making is a mandate.* Jesus did not give the Great Commission, His command to make disciples, as an option to be considered but a mandate to be obeyed. He is our Commander-in-Chief. We are His soldiers. He is our Master. We are His servants. He is our Leader. We are His followers. He is our Shepherd. We are His sheep. He is our Sovereign. We are His subjects. In view of these relationships, we must bow to His will and obey His command to make disciples. However, knowing that He loves us, it is not just a responsibility to obey Him, but also a privilege and a joy.

♦ *Realize that disciple making cannot fail.* Because Jesus possesses all authority, we can be confident as we obey Him.

He said even the gates of Hades would not overcome His church (Matthew 16:18). We cannot step beyond the scope of His authority when we make disciples. Whether we cross the street to disciple a neighbor or cross an ocean to disciple a nation, His authority supports us.

A truck driver may look strong and burly, whereas a letter carrier may look thin and light, but a truck driver had better not bully a letter carrier. The letter carrier has the full power of the United States Government behind him. Even Satan trembles when a follower of Jesus, supported by all authority in heaven and on earth, makes disciples.

♦ *Refuse to be apathetic.* It is often hard to regulate the temperature *in* a church to everyone's liking. It is always too hot for some but too cold for others. However, regulating the temperature *of* the church is even harder. Many members of the congregation are lukewarm, and some are cold. The lukewarm shrug their shoulders at the thought of making disciples, while the cold shake their heads and flatly say no. Both groups shirk their responsibility and displease the Lord, but He delivers a stern rebuke to the lukewarm. He says, "I know your deeds, that you are neither cold nor hot. I wish you were either one or the other! So, because you are lukewarm—neither hot nor cold—I am about to spit you out of my mouth" (Revelation 3:15, 16). The Lord's counsel is " . . . be earnest, and repent" (verse 19). He promises that He will give to everyone who stamps out apathy "the right to sit with me on my throne" (verse 21).

♦ *Realign your values if they do not square with eternal values.* The nation gasped when Enron's stock plummeted and many employees saw their 401K funds vanish. A flood of financial advice soon poured from newspapers, radio stations, and television networks cautioning investors to diversify and take charge of their 401Ks. The rising rate of unemployment coupled with the warning bells ringing loudly from Enron and other companies alerted us to the fact that financial security is not very secure after all. Terrorism also set off some alarms that jolted us. We became aware of the uncertainty of life. After 9-11-02, many Americans, unaccustomed to attending church, filed into pews, hoping to find solace, strength, and a grasp of the eternal. Family ties grew tighter, material things became less important, and spiritual concerns deepened.

Each of us should examine our values from time to time in the light of Jesus' teachings. We can appreciate the comforts of a nice house and a smooth-riding car, but only a personal relationship with Jesus brings comfort to the soul and peace with God. We may pride ourselves on our ability to earn a good income, but our income is not nearly important as the outcome of our eternal destiny. We cannot carry our investment earnings into heaven, but we can build an investment portfolio there in advance of our arrival. Jesus taught, "Do not store up for yourselves treasures on earth, where moth and rust destroy, and where thieves break in and steal. But store up for yourselves treasures in heaven, where moth and rust do not destroy, and where thieves do not break in and steal" (Matthew 6:19, 20).

To illustrate the uncertainty of riches and the folly of wrapping our lives with dollars, gold, CDs, stocks, and bonds, Jesus told about a certain rich farmer. He said the farmer's land yielded such a bumper crop that the farmer decided to tear down his barns to make room for bigger ones. He planned to store all his grain and goods in the new barns and settle down to a life of ease, eating, and entertainment. Little did he know when he put his confidence in material things that his soul was about to enter eternity. God said to him, "You fool! This very night your life will be demanded from you. Then who will get what you have prepared for yourself" (Luke 12:20). Jesus concluded, "This is how it will be with anyone who stores up things for himself but is not rich toward God" (verse 21).

The Lord identified life's highest value as the salvation of even one soul. He asked, "What good is it for a man to gain the whole world, yet forfeit his soul. Or what can a man give in exchange for his soul?" (Mark 8:36, 37). The believer who makes just one disciple recovers a treasure worth more than all the gold, silver, platinum, rubies, and diamonds in the world. As a matter of fact, the treasure of one new disciple is worth more than the whole world. What, then, deserves a higher place in our value system than the work of making disciples?

◆ *Remember the Lord is with you always.* Perhaps you recall your first day on the job at a new workplace. Everything seemed strange and somewhat foreboding. You felt all alone and so unfamiliar with procedures and expectations. You could hardly wait for closing time, but the clock seemed to be frozen. If only someone had been alongside to guide and encourage you every moment of the day! Fortunately, we are never alone as we do the work of making disciples. From the first moment of the first day "on the job" until we turn in our report in heaven, the Lord accompanies us. He promised to be with us "always, to the very end of the age" (Matthew 28:20).

RECOGNIZE THE HARVEST FIELD!

Jesus and His disciples had journeyed from Judea to Samaria. They were tired, thirsty, and hungry when they came to a town called Sychar. The disciples entered the town to get a bite to eat, but Jesus sat down beside a nearby well. It was high noon. Hardly the best time to draw water from a well. After all, who would want to work in the blazing heat of the noonday sun? Certainly, none of the women in the town—except one. A woman of bad reputation arrived at the well when Jesus was there.

"Will you give me a drink?" Jesus asked her. The request started an intense conversation that convinced the woman that Jesus was the Messiah. Then the disciples returned.

Leaving her water jar, the woman ran into town, and excitedly said to the people, "Come, see a man who told me everything I ever did. Could this be the Christ?" (John 4:29).

As the people were making their way to the well, the disciples urged Jesus to eat some of the food they had brought from town. But He declined the offer and instructed them to open their eyes and look at the harvest fields. "They are ripe for harvest," He said (verse 35).

What did Jesus mean by harvest fields? He was speaking figuratively about the people coming from the town to meet Him. The harvest has not changed. It is still people wherever we meet them.

Have followers of Jesus in the United States fallen into
the trap of thinking that only a faraway country is a harvest
field and only missionaries qualify to work in the harvest?
Do we need to rethink our position? Although Nigeria, Tai-
wan, the Philippines, Brazil, and France are harvest fields,
so are Niagara Falls, Toledo, Philadelphia, the Bronx, and
Fresno. Harvest fields exist wherever we are. Our neighborhood, our community, our workplace, our schools, the grocery store, the mall, the gym, the golf course, the tennis
club, and the hospital are all harvest fields. The big question is not, "Where can I go to find a harvest field?" but
"What am I doing to reap a harvest where I am?" Perhaps
we, too, need to obey the instruction Jesus gave His disciples, "Open your eyes and look at the fields."

A church leader analyzed his congregation as consist-
ing of people focused on themselves. "They are not inter-
ested in the Great Commission," he observed, "they want
to be entertained and made to feel good about themselves." If his description is accurate and true of very many
congregations, we need to stop looking at our own needs
and desires and look at the needs of the harvest. Jesus said,
"The harvest is plentiful, but the workers are few. Ask the
Lord of the harvest, therefore, to send out workers into
his harvest field. Go!" (Luke 10:2, 3a).

REV UP YOUR LOVE!

In his January, 2002, State of the Union address, President George Bush called for Americans to donate time and
resources to volunteer work. He suggested that neighbors
help neighbors and people give two years of their life to vol-

unteerism. For the most part the work of making disciples will not be accomplished by salaried church staff but by volunteers, believers who love Jesus. Love, after all, is the most essential qualification for disciple making. Jesus asked Peter three times, "Do you love me? Then He commissioned him to "feed my lambs," "take care of my sheep," and "feed my sheep" (see John 21:15-17).

The apostle Paul, too, identified love as the most essential qualification for disciple making. He wrote, "If I speak in the tongues of men and angels, but have not love, I am only a resounding gong or a clanging cymbal (1 Corinthians 13:1)." He also wrote that faith, hope, and love remain. "But the greatest of these is love" (verse 13), he insisted.

"Love makes labor light," someone wisely observed. We can see that principle applied in a number of situations. Love of country drives a soldier to train hard, work hard, and put his life on the line. Love for his wife motivates a husband to keep his nose to the grindstone five days a week. Because a wife loves her husband, she contributes her skills and energies to the marriage. Love moves a parent to work long and hard to nurture and educate the kids. When love motivates us to work hard, reaching the goal puts the work into perspective. We conclude it was a privilege to work.

What better goal can we have than that of completing the work of making disciples? It is, after all, a goal Jesus set for us. A coach who sets a marathon runner's goal of crossing the finish line in less than two hours rejoices when the runner succeeds. So does the runner. Similarly, Jesus and we, His followers, share the joy when we reach the goal of making disciples.

The 2002 Winter Olympics, held in Salt Lake City, Utah, were preceded by the relaying of the Olympic flame from the East Coast to Salt Lake City. Typically, a torchbearer carried the flame for two tenths of a mile before passing it on to the next person. Most torchbearers ran the distance; others walked. Some ran, jumped, twirled, and danced. But overwhelming joy could be read on the faces of all who carried the torch. Spectators who lined the route also radiated their joy, as they shouted, applauded, cheered, and waved American and Olympic flags. When interviewed, torchbearers spoke of the privilege of being nominated to carry the Olympic flame, and spectators expressed sheer delight at witnessing the spectacle at least once in their lifetime.

Jesus has entrusted His followers with the privilege and responsibility of carrying the light of His teachings across America and the world. We must not fail Him. Thousands along the way are waiting for the light. Some may have only one opportunity in their lifetime to see it.

ROLL UP YOUR SLEEVES!

The apostle Peter challenged us in 1 Peter 1:13 to prepare our minds for action. The original language (Greek) summoned the first-century readers to get ready for action by gathering up their long, flowing garments and tying them between their legs. Doing so would keep them from tripping and would give them greater mobility. Today we would interpret Peter's challenge to mean, "Roll up your sleeves and get to work!"

Clem rolled up his sleeves and got to work. A burly 50-year-old building contractor, Clem made it clear to every new employee that he was a believer. Not only did he tell them he was a believer, he demonstrated this fact by paying decent wages and treating every employee with respect. Furthermore, Clem was available to listen to his employees' concerns, both personal and work-related. He taught a men's weekly Bible class at his church, and not surprisingly welcomed a number of his employees into the class.

When Phil lived in Chicago, he attended a church on the north side, not far from low-income housing projects. He was single, in his early 20s, and separated from his fiancée by several hundred miles. Finding that he had lots of spare time, Phil visited the projects and gained parents' permission to take their children to Sunday school and bring them home promptly. Before long, the congregation anticipated Phil's arrival at Sunday school with 10 to 15 boys and girls tagging along behind him. Phil's sleeves were rolled up for the work of making disciples.

Every Monday is baking day at Joan's house. When her husband of 48 years died of cancer, she received comfort from Christian friends who visited her often. They shared a few verses of Scripture with her, prayed, and brought muffins or cookies. Sometimes they took her to lunch. Following her bereavement, Joan chose to show elderly widows in the community the same loving care she had received. So she began baking muffins and cookies every Monday and delivering them to widows the next day. She is still doing so. Her visits include a brief prayer, her reading a few verses of Scripture, warm conversation, a coffee break or lunch out. Joan's sleeves are rolled up as she makes disciples in her community.

The God who created us gave us the gift of creativity. We see this marvelous gift applied in technology, entertainment, the arts, literature, religion, and business. Without creativity, there would be no Disney World, computers, art museums, a wide variety of church structures, IBM or GE, 747s or space shuttles, digital TV, Internet, SUVs or mini-vans or sedans, *Othello* or *War and Peace* or *Cat in the Hat* or *Tom Sawyer*. Followers of Jesus can tap into their creativity and devise effective ways of discipling others. The mix from which disciple-making creativity springs into action is the willingness to obey Jesus' command to make disciples and a love for Him and for those who need to know Him.

A young mother, Beverly, called every residential number listed in her city's telephone directory and shared her excitement about becoming a follower of Jesus.

Fifteen-year-old Steve arranged to be interviewed during an intermission of a late-night TV showing of a movie. He invited viewers to attend upcoming evangelistic meetings to be held at his church.

A shut-in believer clipped newspaper reports of people seriously affected by car accidents, life-threatening illness, or natural disaster. Then she wrote to them, offering a Scripture promise and her pledge to pray for them.

Making disciples does not require the ability to write and deliver a sermon. The significant work of sharing Jesus' teachings with others can be performed in simple ways and with simple words. We can do more than make disciples, but nothing else is more significant.

Interactive Discipleship

ANSWER THE FOLLOWING QUESTIONS:

1. How did you become a follower of Jesus?

2. It has been said that only what is done for Christ in this life will last. Why do you agree or disagree with this statement?

3. Do you believe a lax attitude about making disciples is widespread? Why or why not?

4. How did Jesus make disciples?

5. If Olympic torchbearers carried the Olympic flame as followers of Jesus carry the light of Jesus' teachings, how long would it take them to carry it coast to coast?

6. Is the Lord with us in the disciple-making task even when we don't feel His presence? Explain.

7. What guarantees our success when we make disciples in obedience to Jesus' command to do so?

8. If you lived in France, where would you begin the work of making disciples? Why?

9. What do you think it would take to disciple the United States in your generation?

10. What creative method will you use to make disciples?

READ WHAT THE FOLLOWING PASSAGES SAY ABOUT THE WORK OF MAKING DISCIPLES:

Isaiah 55:6-13; Jonah 4; Matthew 28:16-20; Luke 5:1-11; Acts 1:1-8; 13:1-3; Romans 1:8-17; I Corinthians 15:1-11; 58; 2 Corinthians 5:14-21; Colossians 1:1-8

MAKE DISCIPLES.

- Share this chapter with a friend.
- Meet with a few Christian friends to brainstorm ways you can make disciples.
- Record your discipling experiences in a diary this week.
- Designate at least two people as a harvest field and pray for them this week.

MULL IT OVER.

Even the best-built house will collapse eventually. The most expensive car will lose its appeal. Money will pass into others' hands. Monuments will crumble. Businesses will fold. Furniture will deteriorate. And high-tech gadgets will become obsolete. But souls are eternal, and the task of making disciples is eternally significant. Proverbs 11:30 points out that "he who wins souls is wise."

REWARDS
THAT LAST
FOREVER

After winning Super Bowl XXXVI, the New England Patriots received a heroes' welcome in Boston. More than 100,000 fans cheered and applauded as the champions paraded through the city. The ensuing rally included jubilant victory speeches and spontaneous dancing. Even the team's owner performed a brief impromptu shuffle.

The weather was chilly and overcast, but the Patriots enjoyed their moment in the sun. They had worked hard all season as a team and had carried their team spirit and work ethic into the big game. As a result, the favored Rams fell to the Cinderella team by a score of 20-17.

A Super Bowl ring and widespread acclaim are fitting rewards for hard work, but they are, after all, only temporal rewards. Eventually the champions will only faintly remember the fans' approving roar, and ultimately their super bowl rings will pass to their beneficiaries. However, life is bigger than a super bowl, and the rewards for a life well spent extend throughout eternity. Jesus promised, "No one who has left home or wife or brothers or parents or children for the sake of the kingdom of God will fail to receive many times as much in this age and, in the age to come, eternal life" (Luke 18:29, 30).

NO EXTENDED WARRANTIES

Whether you purchase a car, a computer, or a copier, you can expect to be asked to add an extended warranty to the transaction. Ironic, isn't it, that a sales person raves about a product's features before you buy it, but after the purchase, rants about the grief you can avoid by taking out an extended warranty? You may just want to scratch your head and wonder, *Hmm. What's wrong with this picture?*

Some things in life have no extended warranty. They may or may not last a lifetime, but they certainly do not extend beyond death. Nevertheless, a person may pour much passion, time, and energy into attaining one or more of those fragile prizes. Wealth, fame, popularity, and even physical fitness are just a few prizes showcased by postmodern society. Although evil does not pounce on everyone who is wealthy or popular or famous or fit or has all of these qualities, it crouches like a hungry tiger ready to devour the unwary. Wealth may fail, as witnessed in bankruptcies. Fame is fleeting. How many twenty-year-olds can identify the Brown Bomber, the Velvet Throat, or the Galloping Horse? Popularity plummets. Movie stars lose their luster. Applauded athletes lose their appeal. And top singers fall out of tune with the times. Fitness eventually gives way to frailty as muscles shrink, bones creak, knees ache, and energy exits. The mind may say, "Go ahead. Lift those weights." But the body says, "No thanks. Lifting myself out of a rocking chair is challenging enough."

Solomon, an extremely wise king, wrote in the Book of Ecclesiastes about a search for satisfaction. He tried everything from the pursuit of knowledge to the pursuit of pleasure but concluded that lasting value comes only from reverencing and obeying God (Ecclesiastes 12:13). He discovered that even a long life brings its share of physical discomfort and weakness. Limbs shake; body stoops; teeth fall out; vision dims; hearing fails; sleep diminishes; fears increase; hair turns white; strength dissipates; and sexual desire disappears (verses 2-5). When life ends, the body returns to the ground and the spirit returns to God (verse 7).

REWARDS THAT LAST FOREVER

If we wisely accept Solomon's wise words about what really matters, we will invest our lives in the pursuit of eternal rewards. Here are just a few that await every obedient follower of Jesus.

♦ *Jesus' approval.* Jesus told about a businessman who conferred with his servants before going out of town. He entrusted each of them with a sum of money. To one he gave five talents (about $7,500); to another, two talents (about $3,000); and to another, one talent (about $1,500).

After a long absence, the businessman returned to find that the servant with five talents had invested them wisely and had increased the money to 10 talents (about $15,000.) The second servant, too, had invested his money wisely and doubled it to four talents (about $6,000). But the third servant had buried his talent. The solitary talent was all he could present to the businessman. His actions met with a stern rebuke from the businessman, whereas the two wise servants received the businessman's approval. The businessman told each of the two, "Well done, good and faithful servant! You have been faithful with a few things; I will put you in charge of many things. Come and share your master's happiness!" (See Matthew 25:21, 23.)

We may conclude from Jesus' words that His approval for work well done includes promotion and perfect happiness. The wise and faithful servants received equal rewards even though their resources differed. Our opportunities to make disciples may be fewer than those of someone with a wider sphere of influence, but the Master will reward us equally on the basis of our faithfulness. First Corinthians 4:2 assures us, "Now it is required that those who have been given a trust must prove faithful."

A mother who crosses the street to disciple a neighbor will be rewarded for her faithfulness to Jesus' command to make disciples, just as a missionary will be rewarded for his faithfulness in crossing an ocean to disciple a nation in obedience to Jesus' command. A schoolteacher who follows Jesus obediently and lets his light shine in a classroom will earn the Master's approval as surely as a faithful senator who shines her light on Capitol Hill. Whether a follower of Jesus teaches two or three children in Sunday school or two or three thousand adults in citywide Bible conferences, faithfulness is the criterion by which the Lord determines rewards.

We must never let the fear of reaping only a small harvest keep us from entering it. Who can predict what might happen in the life of just one person we disciple? The Lord may use him or her to disciple thousands. Dwight L. Moody's Sunday school teacher was a rather timid man, who believed the Lord wanted him to speak to young Dwight about his eternal destiny. So he entered the shoe store where Dwight worked, took him aside, and shared the message of Jesus' love and forgiveness with him. Dwight, who trusted in Jesus as his Savior that day, became a powerful and obedient maker of disciples in Europe as well as the United States. To this day, Moody Bible College in Chicago, an institution founded by Mr. Moody, trains young men and women for the work of discipling others worldwide. If we give the Lord an obedient heart, He can use us however He chooses to make disciples near and far.

• *The crown of life.* In his letter to the church in Smyrna, Jesus foretold persecution, but He encouraged His followers at Smyrna to be "faithful, even to the point of death" (Revelation 2:10a). He promised the faithful, "I will give you the crown of life" (verse 10b).

Very few people get to wear a crown in this life. A sovereign wears a crown. A beauty queen gets to wear one. But how many sovereigns and beauty queens do you know? (Incidentally, the first Miss America contest was held in 1921 and the winner was 5-feet-1-inch tall and weighed 108 pounds.) By contrast, every faithful follower of Jesus will wear a crown someday.

The word Jesus used for "crown" is *stephanos*. It identifies a wreath to be worn around the head. The *stephanos* was presented to a returning military hero or to a triumphant athlete at the Greek games. This crown of victory was a garland woven of oak, of parsley, of ivy, of myrtle, of olive leaves, or of violets or roses. Of course, the *stephanos* would fade and disintegrate, but the apostle Paul wrote in I Corinthians 9:25 about the faithful disciple's *stephanos* as unfading and never disintegrating.

In early television history a popular show captured the attention of American households. "Queen for a Day" dressed the winning contestant in a royal robe, placed a crown on her head, awarded her with prizes, and surrounded her with attendants. But, as the show suggested, the honor lasted only a day. "Who wants to be a crowned victor for eternity?" seems to be a key question posed by the Bible to Jesus' followers. We can answer, "I do," by obeying Jesus' command to make disciples.

♦ *The crown of rejoicing.* The apostle Paul could have gone far in any chosen career. Before becoming Jesus' follower, he earned high marks among the Pharisees and other Jewish leaders as an energetic, ambitious, brilliant, devoted, and intensely loyal Pharisee. While still in his youth, he held membership in the elite Sanhedrin, a ruling body of 70 men. Today, young men with similar characteristics would be climbing corporate ladders at breakneck speed or capture strategic political appointments. But when the young Pharisee we know as Paul became a follower of Jesus, he channeled all his energy, ambition, brilliance, devotion, and loyalty into the work of making disciples. Armed with spiritual gifts, dedicated natural talent and ability, and the power of the Holy Spirit, Paul shook the Roman Empire with the life-changing message of Jesus. People in city after city believed and lined up with him on the side of righteousness. One of those cities was Philippi.

Later, when Paul wrote to the believers at Philippi, he called them, "my joy and crown" (Philippians 4:1). Again, the word translated "crown" is *stephanos*, the victor's crown. Clearly, many lives of new disciples intertwined to form Paul's beautiful crown of rejoicing. A similar crown awaits every follower of Jesus who disciples others.

Aspen, Colorado, has been called the playground of the rich and famous. This Rocky Mountain playground features lots of sunshine, deep-blue skies, eye-catching ski slopes, and multi-million-dollar homes. Several of those high-priced homes were owned by Enron's chairman until his company crashed with all the devastation of an Aspen skier flying into a stand of pine trees at breakneck speed. Whatever happiness those homes brought their owner lasted only a brief time. Material comforts cannot deliver endless happiness or eternal joy. Whether we live in a mud hut or a mansion, drive a Cadillac or a clunker, wear designer clothes or hand-me-downs, we can find real happiness and joy only in what is eternal.

The apostle Paul understood that souls live beyond the grave, whereas stuff—even million-dollar stuff—gets left behind. So he invested his life in eternal work, the work of making disciples. He cherished those whom he discipled on earth and he anticipated seeing them in heaven. They were his "joy and crown"!

Daniel Webster observed:

> *If we work upon marble, it will perish.*
>
> *If we work upon brass, time will efface it.*
>
> *If we rear temples, they will crumble to dust.*
>
> *But if we work upon immortal souls,*
>
> *And embue them with just principles,*
>
> *the fear of God, and the love of*
>
> *their fellow men, we engrave on*
>
> *those tablets that which will brighten all eternity.*

• *The crown of glory.* The apostle Peter wrote to believers who experienced harsh persecution. Enemies of the Truth had uprooted Peter's readers from their homes and native lands. Those loyal followers of Jesus had lost houses and property and jobs in the process, but Peter assured them eternal compensation awaited them. He wrote, "Praise be to the God and Father of our Lord Jesus Christ! In his great mercy he has given us new birth into a living hope through the resurrection of Jesus Christ from the dead, and into an inheritance that can never perish, spoil or fade—kept in heaven for you . . . ." (I Peter 1:3, 4).

Later in I Peter, the apostle addressed those who were in positions of spiritual leadership. He urged them to disciple others faithfully, and to set a strong example for them. He promised that faithful discipleship would please the Lord and gain an eternal reward. "And when the Chief Shepherd appears," Peter wrote, "you will receive the crown of glory that will never fade away" (5:4).

Olympic medal winners deserve the glory they receive. When they stand on pedestals and accept the medals, tears of joy may glisten on their cheeks. They know that all their hard work and rigid discipline paid off. They and their admiring countrymen savor the victory and the awards ceremony. Can you picture the moment in heaven, when Jesus, the Lord of glory, presents His faithful followers with crowns of glory? The glory of Olympic medals pales in comparison with crowns of glory, but like Olympic medals, crowns of glory will prove the indescribable worth of all the discipline and effort that went into the making of disciples.

Sometimes, Olympic judges and spectators disagree about first-place winners. Such a disagreement arose at Salt Lake City, the site of the 2000 Winter Olympic Games, regarding the pairs figure skating competition. The Russians, Elena Berezhnaya and Anton Sikharulidze, were highly favored to win the gold, but their long program fell below expectations. At one point, Anton Sikharulidze faltered after the pair's second jump. Then the Canadian pair, Jamie Sale and David Pelletier, took the ice, and thrilled the audience with a flawless and beautiful performance. The audience rose to their feet and gave the Canadian skaters a standing ovation. The announcers voiced their conviction that the Canadians had claimed the gold and ended 10 years of Russian "gold mining" in the Olympic Games pairs competition. However, when the judges posted their scores, the honor of first place fell to the Russians by a one-judge margin. The audience booed, the TV announcers sat in stunned disbelief, and the Canadian pair registered shock and deep disappointment.

NBC announcer Scott Hamilton, a highly respected champion skater, asked, "How did that happen?" He added, "(Sale and Pelletier) won that. There's not a doubt for anyone in the place except a few judges."

A second announcer, Sandra Bezic, commented, "My heart breaks, and I'm embarrassed for our sport [figure skating]."

As we all know, the vast majority of judges of athletic competition are honorable, trustworthy, and accurate, but faulty judgment sometimes occurs. When it does, the best athletes may not receive the honor they deserve. Fortunately, an unprecedented decision a few days later reversed the earlier one and Sale and Pelletier received their gold medals along with the Russian pair.

Even in our legal system sometimes judges sworn to uphold the law violate it or render faulty decisions. However, followers of Jesus will never receive a faulty review of their life's work. They will never lose the "gold" they deserve. Jesus, who will inspect every believer's works, cannot administer faulty judgment. He is absolutely fair and knowledgeable. The apostle Paul described Jesus as "the righteous Judge" (2 Timothy 4:8).

REWARDS NOW

Although obedient followers of Jesus can anticipate receiving eternal rewards in heaven, they may enjoy significant rewards now. Let's catalog a few of them.

♦ *Jesus' constant companionship.* If you are like most people, perhaps 99.9 percent of the population, you value good relationships. You appreciate your friends, especially those you can confide in—friends who will stand by you when life circumstances turn against you. And in turn you extend loyalty to them. Jesus is the best friend we can have. He said, "Remain in me, and I will remain in you" (John 15:4). He was speaking figuratively about our opportunity to be spiritually productive by drawing sustenance from Him, the Vine. Also, He promised in Matthew 28:28 to accompany us in our disciple-making mission—everywhere we go (to "all nations"), every moment of every day ("always"), and forever ("to the very end of the age").

Acts, chapter 7, relates the account of Stephen's martyrdom. A member of the first-century church in Jerusalem, Stephen fell into the hands of a militant council of Jews bent on destroying all disciple-making efforts. Undaunted, Stephen shared Old Testament history and prophecy as proof that Jesus was the Messiah. His bold witness stirred the council's vehement rage. Teeth gnashed, nostrils flared, and tempers boiled. But calmly, Stephen raised his eyes to heaven and declared that he saw Jesus standing at the Father's right hand (verses 55, 56). The council's rage erupted like an exploding volcano. Its members dragged Stephen out of the city (being religious, they didn't want to kill him inside the holy city!) and stoned him to death. But before he died, Stephen fell to his knees and prayed—not for personal deliverance but for his murderers (verse 60).

No doubt Stephen's courage was bolstered by the knowledge that Jesus was standing by and was ready to welcome him to heaven. This same courage fortifies us, too, as we share His teachings with others, some of whom may oppose us adamantly. Knowing that He is with us, we need not fear.

♦ *Assurance that Jesus hears our prayers.* Stephen knew that Jesus was only a prayer away, and we, too, can know that He is only a prayer away. Having direct access to Jesus outstrips the value of even the best cell phone plan. Prayer is always a local call, the line is never busy, we can call during any day, at night, and on weekends, and we can call as often as we like. Best of all, an answer to each call is guaranteed.

There is one catch, though. Our prayer-call requests must conform to our Lord's will. "If we ask anything according to his will, he hears us" (1 John 5:14). Fortunately, knowing His will is not that difficult. The Bible reveals what He wants us to be and what He wants us to do. It prominently displays the fact that He wants us to make disciples and be His witnesses (see Matthew 28:18-20; Acts 1:8).

♦ *Peace and joy.* As we have seen already in this book, Jesus' peace and joy flood the mind and heart of every obedient disciple. His peace "transcends all understanding" and will guard our hearts and minds (Philippians 4:7). His joy is complete, and no one can steal it from us (John 16:22, 24). Hardships may befall us as we make disciples, but our peace and joy can remain full and undisturbed.

According to William Barclay, John Nelson reported

on a disciple-making mission he and John Wesley con-
ducted in Cornwall, England. "All that time, Mr. Wesley
and I lay on the floor: he had a greatcoat for a pillow, and
I had Burkitt's notes on the New Testament for mine. After being here near three weeks, one morning about three
o'clock Mr. Wesley turned over, and, finding me awake,
clapped me on the side, saying: 'Brother Nelson, let us be
of good cheer; I have one whole side yet, for the skin is off
but on one side!'" One morning the two were returning
from a meeting in which John Wesley's preaching had been
very powerful. Nelson relates, "As we returned, Mr. Wesley stopped his horse to pick the blackberries, saying,
'Brother Nelson, we ought to be thankful that there are
plenty blackberries; for this is the best country I ever saw
for getting a stomach, but the worst I ever saw for getting
food!'" (*The Letters to the Philippians, Colossians, and Thessalonians*, The Saint Andrew Press, 1960, pp. 64, 65). The
Lord's peace made Wesley content and His joy enabled
him to maintain a rich sense of humor even in difficult
times. Making disciples was worth more to him than a
cozy bed and abundant food.

♦ *The satisfaction of knowing you are performing life's
greatest work.* If the President of the United Sates appointed you to a Cabinet position, wouldn't you feel honored? What greater satisfaction could you possibly
experience than that of serving your nation at the request
of the man in the Oval office? The answer is, discipling
your nation at the command of the Lord of heaven and
earth.

We don't have to be preachers to disciple others. Each

of us can perform the task in simple, everyday ways: by acts of kindness; by speaking wholesome, edifying words; by telling others who Jesus is, what He taught, and why He died and rose again; by helping the poor and needy; by working honestly; by keeping our promises; by writing letters to the editor in defense of morality and righteousness; by giving to the Lord's work; and by setting the right example.

Our nation doesn't lack congregations; it has about 350,000. But each of those congregations needs men and women who will obey Jesus' command to make disciples. The silent majority must become the vocal majority, proclaiming Jesus' Word courteously but boldly, plainly but effectively, and soberly but joyfully. Our nation can become a discipled nation in our generation. However, for that to happen we need to hear the Lord's appeal, "Whom shall I send? And who will go for us?" and answer as Isaiah did, "Here am I. Send me!" (Isaiah 6:8).

The work of discipleship is imperative, and the rewards are incomparable!

Interactive Discipleship

ANSWER THE FOLLOWING QUESTIONS:

1. What is the most treasured award you have received? How does it compare with the rewards Jesus gives His loyal followers?

2. What do you prize most in life?

3. What do you think others prize most in life?

4. If no rewards were given in heaven, would you still follow Jesus faithfully? Why or why not?

5. How can you persuade those who know you best to follow Jesus?

6. What do you think it might take to awaken the church—the sleeping giant—to engage vigorously in the work of making disciples?

7. How can you invest more time in disciple-making?

8. What rewards for making disciples do you see that aren't cited in this chapter?

9. How can you keep eternal values in mind when you make important choices?

10. What letter grade would you assign to your current disciple-making efforts? To your future efforts?

READ WHAT THE FOLLOWING PASSAGES SAY ABOUT REWARDS:

Genesis 15:1-7; Psalm 18:20-30; 58:1-11; 84:8-12; Daniel 12:1-3; Luke 6:27-36; I Corinthians 3:10-15; 5:1-10; Hebrews 11:1-6; Revelation 22:7-16

MAKE DISCIPLES.

- Share this chapter with a friend.
- Tell someone about a difficulty you overcame because you knew the Lord stood by you.

- Ask three friends why no one should entrust their eternal well-being to material possessions?
- Write a brief poem or a description of heaven and share it with a loved one.

MULL IT OVER.

"In the strength of the Lord let me labor and pray,
Let me watch as a winner of souls;
That bright stars may be mine in that glorious day,
When His praise like the sea billow rolls.
Will there be any stars, any stars in my crown
When at evening the sun goeth down?
When I wake with the blest in the mansions of rest,
Will there be any stars in my crown?"

—ELIZA E. HEWITT

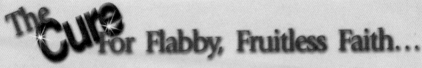

The Cure for Flabby, Fruitless Faith...
...A DISCIPLED NATION PLAN

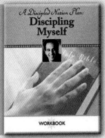

LEARNING TO FOLLOW CHRIST IN OUR DAILY LIVES & GROWING SPIRITUALLY

A Discipled Nation Plan: **Discipling Myself** — WORKBOOK

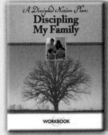

A Discipled Nation Plan: **Discipling My Family** — WORKBOOK

ESTABLISHING LOVING FAMILY RELATIONSHIPS & TEACHING OUR FAMILIES HOW TO FOLLOW CHRIST

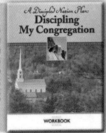

SUPPORTING OUR PASTORS & EQUIPPING MEMBERS TO "EACH ONE BRING ONE EACH YEAR"

A Discipled Nation Plan: **Discipling My Congregation** — WORKBOOK

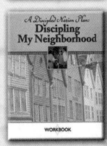

A Discipled Nation Plan: **Discipling My Neighborhood** — WORKBOOK

REACHING NEIGHBORS THROUGH RELATIONSHIPS & SHOWING LOVE IN EFFECTIVE WAYS

FOR SMALL GROUPS, SUNDAY SCHOOL, AND ONE-ON-ONE MENTORING
PARTICIPANT WORKBOOKS PROVIDE CHALLENGES THAT "PUT FEET TO OUR FAITH!"
LEADER'S GUIDES HELP THE LEADER START DISCUSSIONS AND BUILD DISCIPLING TEAMS!
PASTOR'S GUIDES HELP PASTORS USE PROGRAM AS A CATALYST FOR CHURCH GROWTH!

"IF EVEN SEVERAL THOUSAND CHRISTIANS IN AMERICA TOOK [A DISCIPLED NATION] COMMITMENTS SERIOUSLY, THE COUNTRY WOULD ALMOST CERTAINLY BE TURNED UPSIDE DOWN BEFORE YOU CAN SAY 'DISCIPLE.'"
JOEL BELZ, CEO, WORLD MAGAZINE

PRICE LIST

ISBN	TITLE	PRICE	ISBN	TITLE	PRICE
1-931774-17-3	A DISCIPLED NATION PLAN (1, 2)	$65.00	1-931744-08-4	DISCIPLING MY CONGREGATION LEADER'S PACK (2)	$22.00
1-931744-00-9	DISCIPLING MYSELF LEADER'S PACK (2)	$15.00	1-931744-09-2	DISCIPLING MY CONGREGATION WORKBOOK	$10.00
1-931744-01-7	DISCIPLING MYSELF WORKBOOK	$10.00	1-931744-12-2	DISCIPLING MY NEIGHBORHOOD LEADER'S PACK (2)	$22.00
1-931744-04-1	DISCIPLING MY FAMILY LEADER'S PACK (2)	$22.00	1-931744-13-0	DISCIPLING MY NEIGHBORHOOD WORKBOOK	$10.00
1-931744-05-X	DISCIPLING MY FAMILY WORKBOOK	$10.00			

(1) CONTAINS ONE OF EACH LEADER'S PACKS
(2) PACKS INCLUDE WORKBOOK, LEADER'S GUIDE, AND PASTOR'S GUIDE

PUBLISHER INFORMATION:
THE AMY FOUNDATION
WWW.ADISCIPLEDNATION.COM
WWW.AMYFOUND.ORG

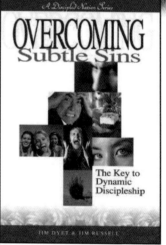